RED,
RED

VE THE
EACHING

ney
r

Rowman & Littlefield Education
Lanham, Maryland • Toronto • Plymouth, UK
2007

Published in the United States of America
by Rowman & Littlefield Education
A Division of Rowman & Littlefield Publishers, Inc.
A wholly owned subsidary of The Rowman & Littlefield Publishing Group, Inc.
4501 Forbes Boulevard, Suite 200, Lanham, Maryland 20706
www.rowmaneducation.com

Estover Road
Plymouth PL6 7PY
United Kingdom

Illustrations by Angelo Sirico

British Library Cataloguing in Publication Information Available

Library of Congress Cataloging-in-Publication Data

Mahoney, Amy Sutton, 1976–
  Untenured, uncensored : how to survive the first years of teaching / Amy
Sutton Mahoney, Christopher Purr.
     p. cm.
  ISBN-13: 978-1-57886-607-6 (hardcover : alk. paper)
  ISBN-13: 978-1-57886-609-0 (pbk. : alk. paper)
  ISBN-10: 1-57886-607-3 (hardcover : alk. paper)
  ISBN-10: 1-57886-609-X (pbk. : alk. paper)
  1. First year teachers—Training of—United States. I. Purr, Christopher,
1971– II. Title.

  LB2844.1.N4M24 2007
  371.1–dc22   2007000380

For our families:
Brian, Brendan, and Patrick Mahoney

and

Tara, James, Amanda, and Erin Purr.

CONTENTS

Acknowledgments   vii

Introduction: Why Am I Reading This Book?   ix

1   Understanding the Mind-set   1

2   Only 175 Days to Go . . . How to Survive the
     First Week of School   19

3   Have You Seen My Grade Book? Getting
     Organized So You Never Have to Ask That
     Dreaded Question   39

4   Behave Yourself! Discipline and the
     New Teacher   55

5   Hello, Mother; Hello, Father (Hello, Nanny;
     Hello, Legal Guardian): Dealing with Parents   69

6   Camaraderie, Competition, Calumny, and
     Coffee Talk: The Politics of the
     Teachers' Lounge   91

CONTENTS

7   And in This Corner . . . School Violence and the
     New Teacher   115

8   Don't Bring Me Down   131

Conclusion   149

ACKNOWLEDGMENTS

We would like to thank Bruce Copper, Ph.D., of Fordham University in New York City. He is an outstanding mentor and writer who knew the exact direction in which to point us!

Our friend and principal, Aaron Trummer, and our friend and administrator (and husband), Brian Mahoney, deserve a great amount of gratitude for their efforts during the "brainstorming" stage and their contributions to the Administrative Analysis sections of the book.

Thanks also to all education and English professors from Siena College of Loudonville, New York, and Queens College and Mercy College of New York City for training us to do the best job in the world.

Thank you to Joe "Pop-Pop" Mahoney, whose countless hours of babysitting allowed time for writing!

Finally, thanks to all of the students, teachers, administrators, and secretaries with whom we have worked over the years, especially those from Mahopac High School. You are our second family!

INTRODUCTION
Why Am I Reading This Book?

I f you are reading this book, you are most probably just starting your journey into the uncharted waters of that most glorious of professions, the one held in such high esteem by our society, teaching. Ah, teaching! The Brass Ring! The Holy Grail! The Dream Job! What other profession allows you to hang out with a bunch of kids during a short workday for an obscenely high salary, bestows some magical-sounding defense against firing called tenure, and provides you with two months off a year so you can lounge about on your yacht on the French Riviera?

In case you weren't able to spot it, the preceding paragraph contained quite a bit of irony. Of course, there are those that view the life of the teacher as being quite undemanding, uncomplicated, and filled with free time. If you are one of those people, you may want to consider looking into another line of work, because nothing can be further from the truth. Except, perhaps, for referring to it as a "dream job."

As we, the authors of this book, have discovered over the years, the rewards that teaching provides cannot be measured in terms of wealth. For those that measure their contributions to society by the size of their weekly paychecks, this can be a difficult concept to grasp. For those capable of finding intellectual satisfaction in other ways, it is a simple fact. Very few people have achieved financial independence through teaching, and that is something that must be understood by the new teacher early on. There will be gains, albeit not financial, that will change your life for the better. The trick is surviving through your first years in order to acquire them. Hopefully this book will be of some assistance in this matter.

What could be so difficult about teaching, you might say? Rest assured, it will be considerably more difficult than you might think and in ways you have most likely not considered. For example, what do you do when you call a child's parent and do not receive the warm reception you were expecting? Or how do you cope with the finger pointing you get after a student saw you with another young teacher of the opposite sex? How should you react if the seasoned veterans you have just joined behave in a less than politically correct way behind closed doors? Just how much should you involve the administration when dealing with difficult students? And, as shocking as it sounds, just how vulnerable are teachers to false accusations of inappropriate behavior? If you think that one's far-fetched, try enforcing a dress code in the middle of June.

These are the day-to-day issues your professors may not have covered in your previous education courses. And who can blame them? How often do they have to deal with pissed-off parents? When is the last time you saw a professor break up a fight between two kids out on the Quad because they had a "beef" with each other? How many times have you observed a professor emeritus politely ask a young woman to tuck her exposed thong back into her jeans? Probably not too often.

As amusing or outrageous as some of these examples may sound, they barely scratch the surface in regard to what a teacher sees on a regular basis. And that, thankfully, is where *Untenured, Uncensored* comes in, for it is written by teachers, for teachers. We've already made the mistakes and endured the awkward encounters you will face over the course of your career. And together, along with commentary from an administrator, we hope to provide you with the advice you will need to emerge from those encounters unscathed. Of course, please note that names and situations have been changed to protect the anonymity of our students and colleagues.

It doesn't matter if you are fresh out of college, changing careers, an "old-timer" looking for some new strategies, or just someone who has an interest in the profession of teaching. Let this book be your road map through the twists and turns of modern education. We will share with you our personal experiences that exemplify the difficulties that await you and how you should deal with them. Hopefully, they will help ease you through those early, difficult years. And who knows? They may even help get you tenure.

1

UNDERSTANDING THE MIND-SET

As new teachers prepare to enter the classroom for the first time, it is vital that they understand the mind-set not only of their students, but of themselves as well. Once you enter that school building, you are entering another world, where you will see and hear things that may shock you. Have you thought about what your students are going to reveal to you about themselves, whether they realize it or not? How do you think you would react if you overheard one of your underachievers talking about how drunk he or she got over the weekend? Or worse yet, what if it was one of your star pupils? What would you do if you knew that the kid would doubtlessly get the beating of a lifetime if his or her parents found out? The issues that will confront you will be much more complex than you realize.

And what about you? Have you thought about what kind of teacher you are going to be? Are you leaning more toward the iron-fisted tyrant or the cool one that wears jeans and spends most of Monday talking about everybody's weekend? On that note, just how much of yourself do you plan to reveal to your students? Do they really need to know that you just got engaged and are having all kinds of trouble finding just the right reception hall? Rest assured that they would much rather listen to you talk about your problems than, say, calculus, but it's not a good habit to get into. This is coming from people who know. Every situation is different, every kid is different, and the sooner you find the answers to these questions the better off you will be.

YOU ABSOLUTELY, POSITIVELY, CANNOT GO HOME AGAIN

It was during a seminar on violence in schools that one of your illustrious authors heard a clear example of why you cannot go home again. The facilitator was a high school principal, and a teacher brought up that he would feel bad if he reported on a student that he really liked or was friendly with for being involved in a fight. The entire countenance of the facilitator changed in a flash. It was as if she just heard that vicious rumor that's been going around about the existence of Santa Claus. Completely dumbfounded. However, being a pro, she did not let the comment stymie her for too long. She looked at the inexperienced young man and, very calmly, said:

> You are not their friend. You can be friendly, but you are not their friend. You are not a kid anymore. You are an adult that has been entrusted with overseeing the education and well-being of other people's children. If a child has been involved in a fight, it is your job to see to it that that child is held accountable for his or her role in it. Remember, you are not exactly the coolest thing in the world. You are a teacher.

Those in attendance with a little more teaching experience under their belts fought hard to suppress the grins that tried to sneak across their faces. You could almost hear the laughter that was going on in their minds, laughter that was not directed at the young teacher, but themselves. The "old-timers" in the room knew exactly what she was trying to say, that they were not the coolest things in the world, probably the furthest thing from it. Of course, that was an understanding that came from experience, which this young gentleman did not have. He was also no doubt suffering from a case of Peter Pan syndrome, in which the sufferer has difficulty making the transition into adulthood. Like it or not, he's a teacher now, not a student. It's time to grow up.

EMBRACE YOUR INNER BALD SPOT

If you want to make the transition from student to teacher a little easier, understand that you have just become what many youngsters revile. The trick is not to let that get to you. You could be the nicest person in the world, and you probably are, but (depending on the type of students you end up with) prepare yourself for a pretty rough time as your students are feeling you out, looking for weaknesses. The hunter has become the hunted. If you don't have a sense of humor, develop one. Fast. Unlike your thoughtful friends and relatives, your students may gladly remind you of the fact that you are going bald every time you turn around to write something on the board. Get ready to find unflattering pictures of yourself drawn in your textbooks. And, yes, prepare yourself to be intensely disliked by some.

Despite all of this gloom and doom, however, remember this: It comes with the territory. Don't take it personally. And it doesn't last forever. Remember, the buck stops with you. You are the one the kids will look at when the fire alarm goes off, so make sure you know the evacuation instructions for your room. Once you come to terms with your role as authority figure, things will become much easier. Of course, getting to that point will take some doing, but now you know what to look for inside your own head. Let's take a look inside a child's.

CHAPTER 1

THEY SAY THE DARNDEST THINGS

Kids live in two worlds. They have the world at home that they share with their family, and then there is that eerie, parallel universe called school, and they like them kept separate. Kids do things in school that they would never dream about doing at home, and for obvious reasons. You were probably no different when you were in school. Can you remember where you dropped your first F-bomb? I bet it wasn't at the dinner table. More than likely it was on a school playground. Do you remember looking forward to going to school so you could meet up with your friends and get down to the important business of gossiping? Of course you do. And you loved it. Your students are going to feel the same way. They enjoy gossiping as much as you did. If something really important is going on, that conversation will follow the kids right into class.

That fact brings up a conundrum that has baffled many an educator over the years: Just how do you get a classroom full of twelve-year-olds to shut the hell up? In order to answer that question, one needs to understand the cause of all that conversation.

Kids enjoy talking to their friends, just like adults do. They want to be noticed, just like adults do. And, on a more serious note, some kids crave attention so much that they will say or do whatever they have to in order to get it. Sadly, this most likely means the child is not getting that attention at home. While you are thinking about that, think about this: How many adults do you know with the same problem? Fitting in and being liked and having fun are things we have to work on our whole lives. Granted, we leave the bullies of middle school behind when we enter adulthood, but what about that bully of a boss you may encounter? Or the crazed hockey parent that didn't like the hit your child just put on his son? Or, even worse, what about a bully at home? At least you have the benefit of more life experience.

Children don't. Bear that in mind when you want to scream at them to be quiet. In fact, try not to scream at all. It's a bad habit to get into. You'll find out why in another chapter.

It is in school that kids learn about socialization. Any other experience they have interacting with others has most likely been at home with relatives. Parents realize this. It used to be you started your child in kindergarten and that was it. Now, waiting for your child to reach preschool age can be seen as irresponsible. "Mommy and Me" activities are becoming the norm. Apparently, it is never too early to start your child off on the road to good social skills, at least for some parents.

Unfortunately, not all parents are as concerned about the social development of their children. As a result, you are going to encounter some students that are outgoing and others that are not. Some will have their hand raised to answer every question. Others will try to burn a hole in their desk with imagined heat vision as they try desperately to avoid your gaze. Your job is to get through to all of them. Not an easy task, I assure you.

THINGS TO WATCH FOR

Don't Judge a Book by Its Cover. Not every kid that wears all black is angry, suicidal, or dangerous. Not every jock is opposed to learning. Not every kid who shaves his or her head is an anti-Semite. Some of the greatest kids you will ever have the pleasure to teach will look like those listed above. Don't misjudge them because they present themselves in an unusual style. In fact, try not to judge them at all.

Understand That You Are No Jerry Seinfeld. As stated earlier, a sense of humor is a prerequisite if you are to survive as a teacher. Just be careful how you use it. We are both major advocates of keeping it light in class. If the kids are smiling, then they are listening and engaged. You've got them right where you want them. If you are not careful, however, you could get a little carried away and something inappropriate may slip out. Professional comedians work very hard at what they do. You are not a professional comedian. And even if you are, you are not on stage. You are in a classroom. Remember that. Have fun, but remember your audience. One more thing to remember: Anything you say can and will be used against you by a disgruntled student. It doesn't matter if you were kidding and everybody in class that day knew it, they're still your words.

Still Waters Run Deep. Don't forget about the quiet ones. Fight the urge to always call on the same kid who always knows the right answer. Get them involved. If they are unresponsive, say hi to them before class. Ask them what's new. Simple stuff like that will show them you care and will bring you a step closer to breaking through the student-teacher barrier. And who knows what treasures you may find in those waters.

The responsibilities at the feet of today's teachers are remarkable. Some that enter our profession seem to delude themselves into thinking that all they are accountable for is punching their card in the morning, teaching their classes, reporting for any duty assignment they might have, and punching out again. They can't be bothered with whatever "problems" the kids might have. Thankfully, we have encountered a scarce few of those people in our experience. Unfortunately, they are out there.

Do yourself a favor: Don't become one of those people. Many of the students you encounter throughout your career are going to have some of the "problems" that the teacher with ice water in his or her veins refuses to deal with. It doesn't matter if you are working in the lowest-achieving district on record or the plushest private school in the world. Neglectful, abusive parents aren't restricted to a particular financial demographic. Teens in the ghetto fall in love as passionately as those that are driven home by a chauffeur. And, sadly, there are people more than willing to peddle drugs and alcohol to our youth in every community. Like it or not, kids will be bringing much more than their homework into your classroom, so be prepared.

CASE STUDIES

Case One: Say What?

I may not be good at sports, but I can make people laugh. It's just something I do. Do I do it because I enjoy making others happy or because I have low self-esteem? I really don't care. What I do know is that I need to have my students as well as myself cracking up while I teach.

On one particular day, I decided to pick on a neighboring town in upstate New York called Pawling. Now Pawling is an absolutely beautiful town with fantastic people living there. It just happens to be slightly more rustic than the town where I teach. For whatever reason, I made some kind of crack about the town of Pawling not having electricity. This elicited a few chuckles from the class and I moved on with my lesson, quickly forgetting that I had even made the comment. When the period was over and the kids filed out of the room, I noticed that one of my ESOL students was still there. And he didn't look happy:

"Mr. Purr, can I talk to you for a minute?"

"Sure. What's up?"

Nothing on earth could have prepared me for what I was about to hear:

"I just wanted you to know that we have electricity in Poland."

Where the hell did that come from? Completely baffled, I tried to continue the conversation:

"Why are you telling me this?"

"I just wanted to tell you that I don't think you are very funny."

After a few moments of looking around for the hidden camera, it finally dawned on me. Poland. Pawling. This kid thinks I made fun of Poland.

"No, no. You misunderstood me. I said Pawling, not Poland. Pawling is a town over in the next county."

He was a pretty big kid, and obviously not a fan of Polish jokes, so I braced myself for the worst as I waited to see if he believed me or not. Finally, he simply said, "Okay." He left the room and we never spoke of it again.

Case Two: Amy Receives Some Unwanted Advice

Not having had very much experience dealing with the adolescent mind prior to my first year of teaching, I did not fully understand the absolute necessity to choose each and every word uttered in their presence with extreme care. Being fresh out of college, I was used to saying just about anything I wanted. The idea had not yet sunk in that kids can easily misinterpret what they hear from an adult, which was a classification I had not fully accepted as pertaining to me. You must remember to think twice about almost everything you say to your students, especially if the conversation revolves around a sensitive topic, and particularly when the sensitive topic is sex.

I was on hall duty one morning during first period, which occurs between 7:30 and 8:30 A.M. That time of day is a bit early for any kind of discussion if you ask me, but obscenely early for the conversation I accidentally became involved in. I was having a nice, innocent chat with some of my favorite twelfth-grade girls, and the topic of conversation eventually became the ongoing dramatic relationship between one of the girls, Rebecca, and her on-and-off boyfriend of four years, Kieran.

Kieran and Rebecca made Ike and Tina and Bill and Monica (and Hillary) look like the poster children for healthy relationships. The only thing that kept them together was Kieran's intolerance of the possibility of Rebecca dating anyone else and Rebecca's willingness to do whatever it took to keep Kieran interested. Needless to say, it had been an interesting four years knowing the two, and I offered many prayers that they would not attend the same college, an idea that had been discussed enthusiastically.

As crazy as I thought their behavior was, I was proud of the fact that I never lost sight of where each one was coming from. While I disagreed with them staying together, I was able to understand it by looking at things from their point of view and I tried to help Rebecca find healthy solutions to her daily crises.

During our first-period discussion, some of the girls were prompting Rebecca to tell me the "outrageous" thing that she did the night before that she was currently regretting. I reminded them that I didn't want to know and the real issue was that she was feeling pressure to behave with Kieran in a way that made her feel uncomfortable, which was a serious matter that needed discussing with her counselor. That was what we were supposed to do, right? Well, one of the young ladies blurted out the news before I could finish my lecture, and I was so shocked and appalled that such a sweet girl would do something so unthinkable that I squealed, "Oh my God, Rebecca! Why would you do that?"

Surprisingly, she didn't seem particularly embarrassed by my shock and very calmly replied, "Well, Mrs. Mahoney, it feels so much better for the guy!"

Obviously, Rebecca and I were not on the same page. I wanted to know why she thought such behavior was a good idea, while she thought I was seeking sex advice. I excused myself, went straight to the computer, and through the miracle of technology sent an e-mail that passed this problem directly to her poor, unfortunate guidance counselor.

Case Three: If You Can't Beat Them . . .

After ten years of teaching, I was starting to develop a pretty high opinion of myself. I had worked in a variety of neighborhoods around New York and ultimately found myself in a relatively up-scale neighborhood just north of the city. I was married, I had a few kids, and more importantly, I was tenured.

There had been quite a bit of hiring by the district during the past few years, and for the first time in my career, I was one of the more veteran teachers in my department. I did not let the fact that I was becoming more and more hairless as the years went by deter me from feeling like a hoary-headed sage for some of my newer colleagues.

People were actually asking me for advice, a responsibility I was not used to, yet accepted with humility. After all, I was the one with all the "inner-city" experience. I had more notches on my gun belt than these kids would ever see outside of a museum. I was more than happy to tell a few tales from the trail when asked about how I dealt with certain issues, particularly discipli-nary ones. The funny thing was that no one seemed to seek my advice on how to actually teach, but, happy for the attention, I wallowed in my role as "hard-ass disciplinarian."

I have never had a school year that I would call "easy." In fact, anyone would be hard-pressed to find a teacher that could say that. Nonetheless, you will experience classes of kids over the years that will be a collective joy, a high-maintenance inconve-nience, or, despite whatever you do to prevent it, a living night-mare.

Through a programming nightmare, I found myself buried un-der a group of seniors in my composition class that absolutely did not belong together. Of course, I was used to difficult kids, but what made this situation different was the fact that they ap-peared to be ready for me too. The shenanigans started early, so "superteacher" leapt immediately into action.

I started out by assigning them seats on the second day of classes. They wailed and moaned about how they were seniors and this was childish, and I smiled as they reluctantly took their new seats. One of my favorite tactics is to seat the most vocal protestors in the front of the room, as they generally turn out to be the ones you have to watch the closest. Others less confident than me would be tempted to seat them in the back of the room and ignore the problem, but, not me, for I was fearless.

The one student who, in my hurried estimation, I thought might prove to be the most challenging landed directly in front of my desk. As I later discovered, "most challenging" became the understatement of the semester, and I wished I could reverse time and allow him to sit in the back of the room where he could generate his mischief as far from me as possible.

One thing that must be said about the boy, who I will call Brian, was that he was very funny. He was obscenely inappropriate, but boy, did he put me in the awkward position of biting my lip at the beginning of each period as I would walk into class and find something new and bizarre on my desk every day. It was mostly artwork, if you could call it that, of a digital nature.

He was quite adept at manipulating images on his computer and each day I would discover a new variation on whatever theme we happened to be studying cleverly positioned on my desk so I would not be able to miss it. Brian always got to class before me as I had a class in another room right before his period, so catching him in the act proved to be a chore. Secretly, however, I hoped I did not catch him because his offerings invariably caused me to chuckle. Later on, I wished I had taken a more serious approach to his antics.

The images were innocent enough and they always seemed to relate to what we were doing, so at first they were no big deal. For example, the day after watching a John Stossel video on free speech, I found the reporter, sans his trademark mustache, holding a glass containing what could only be an alcoholic beverage, clad in a pair of red pajamas and sporting a set of antlers. As Christmas was only a few weeks away, it was both funny and topical. I did my best to contain my mirth, but I burst out laughing at the sight of the lauded newsman in such a state. And that was the moment I opened the door for more daily gifts, gifts the majority of the class started participating in.

Growing up with a last name like "Purr" is going to lead to inevitable consequences for the one who bears it, so it is something you must learn to deal with unless you intend to change it. Naturally, I eventually started finding pictures of cats on my desk. They started out harmless enough, like the one of Mr. Stossel's head on a cat's body. Unfortunately, they got more and more inappropriate as the days went on. In fact, the thought of some of them still causes me to blush, so I will not describe them here. Rest assured, however, as they pertained to cats, an animal often called by another name, there were plenty of things Brian could do creatively with this subject.

One problem I did not have with that class was lateness, because these kids absolutely bolted to class to see my reaction to Brian's latest daily creation. Knowing full well who the culprit was, yet still unable to catch him in the act, I finally told the class that the pictures were starting to become inappropriate and that the person responsible was going to have to stop. I added this final picture to my growing collection of evidence and moved on with the lesson. And then the meowing started.

They were supposed to be reading an essay. About five minutes after my lecture about the pictures, I heard the first one. I looked up and tried in vain to catch the culprit, but I had no chance. No problem, I thought. I'm the one with all the experience, remember? I decided to roll my eyes and ignore the juvenile behavior. Naturally, there were a few more meows that followed, but I wasn't going to let that get to me. I wasn't going to let them have the satisfaction of seeing me lose it and start screaming at the class to stop meowing. They would understand how childishly they were behaving and would cut it out on their own. Except they didn't stop it. Instead, it started to get worse. Kids that ordinarily were quiet as, well, mice, suddenly started getting in on the act. I saw things beginning to get out of control, so I had to intervene: "Okay, guys. That's enough." This resulted in peals of laughter from the group. One of Brian's minions decided to get some time in the spotlight: "What's the matter, Mr. Purr? Don't you like cats?"

More laughter. And the really sad part was the fact that meowing isn't particularly funny. I could take a well-thought-out joke, but this was ridiculous. Instead of quieting down, a surreal sort of free association started to occur from random kids throughout the room:

"Hey, Mr. Purr, do you have any cat food?"

"Look, it's raining cats and dogs outside."

"Do any of you girls feel like getting into a cat fight?"

"Meow!"

I tried to hunker down and weather the storm as the clock moved ever so slightly toward the end of the period. Up until this point, the comments were fairly harmless, so I decided to let them have their period of nonsense, as my biology teacher allowed me to do once when I was in the eighth grade. Of course, Brian couldn't do a little harmless stand-up like I tried to do when I was twelve. Instead, he had to turn his comment up to eleven: "Oh! I just remembered! I have to go home and shave my (insert synonym for cat that begins with P)."

Brian's mother was more than receptive on the phone and swore that her son would cut out both the comments and the unwanted picture deliveries. Naturally, he did not, and my future calls were answered by her machine. Brian went through a few periods of out-of-school suspension that gave me a much-needed break but did little as far as rehabilitation. His defiance only emboldened the rest of the class, and soon, I was met with another ridiculous question on a daily basis: "Mr. Purr, can you take us to see *Cats*?"

The latest obsession with this class was for me to take them on a field trip to Broadway to see the Andrew Lloyd Webber musical *Cats*. The fact that *Cats* was no longer running on Broadway did not deter them; in fact, it only seemed to inspire them more. I arrived one day to find a stack of permission slips, on school letterhead and using the appropriate language, to see *Cats* sitting on my desk. The class erupted into laughter. I had called parents, thrown kids out, and, yes, even resorted to yelling, but to no avail. While some of the more responsible kids responded, there were just too many kids that either didn't care what happened to them or were so deviously subtle that punishment was difficult to hand out.

Before I knew it, the date of the trip that was not really a trip was just a day away. The kids were asking me if they should bring lunch or money to spend at a restaurant. They were taking this role-play very seriously. It felt very much like a competition, one I did not want to lose.

I was now the one walking into the English office with my head down and receiving consolation from the newcomers. Where had I gone wrong? I had been teaching for ten years! This shouldn't have been happening to me. It was at one of these low moments that I got some help from an unlikely source, a new teacher: "Chris, how has your sixth-period class been going?" The circle was now complete. When I left her I was the master. Now I was the learner: "Not good. Nothing seems to be working. And the worst part is they're actually funny! Half the time I want to laugh and the other half I want to strangle them!"

Leave it to the newbie to point me in the direction of the obvious: "So why don't you just go with it?"

I looked at her, puzzled: "What do you mean?"

"Well, even though they aren't very well behaved, they sound pretty clever. Maybe you should try being clever as well."

I thought I was being clever by giving seniors assigned seating. I thought I was being clever by ignoring an obnoxious behavior and hoping that it would magically go away. It turned out I wasn't being clever at all. I was resting on my so-called laurels. Her comments caused me to do something I hadn't done in several years: be creative.

After scouring the area that night and coming in extra early the following morning to use the copier, I actually looked forward to my class of feline lovers. When they arrived I welcomed them at the door and urged them to refrain from smoking and to turn off their cell phones. They were quite taken aback by my unusual behavior. When the late bell rang and they were all seated, I asked them to sit back and enjoy the show. And with that, I turned off the lights and popped in the DVD of a staged version of *Cats* I had found in a video store two counties over.

Of course, I had spent the rest of the previous evening typing up an assignment to go along with it. When the credits rolled and *Cats* appeared on the screen, the class erupted into raucous cheering and clapping, enough to cause a nearby teacher to come into the room and make sure I was okay. Of course, the kids had a field day making fun of the spandex-clad performers and the thrusting that was such a major part of their choreography, and I let them. At the end of the period, I received a plethora of thanks for taking them on the imaginary trip. The last student to leave was Brian. I looked at him and waited for his reaction. It was very simple: "That was funny."

The rest of the term was much better.

ADMINISTRATIVE ANALYSIS

Case One

What Chris experienced is a perfect example of what can go wrong when you try to joke around with your students. There is absolutely nothing wrong with keeping the atmosphere in your class light as long as that levity is not getting in the way of learning. Just be very careful with what you say. It doesn't matter that the student misunderstood the word Chris said. What does matter is the fact that the student was offended by something his teacher said, something that was not part of that day's lesson.

You take a pretty big risk when you try to act like a comedian in class. You never know what is going to offend someone. This case was based on a misunderstanding, but it still could have offended a student that might have had ties to that town. Overall, I must say that Chris used poor judgment in this situation. To reiterate, telling a joke now and then is fine, just as long as you think it through a little before you say it.

Case Two

Amy's first mistake was falling into the habit of chatting it up with a group of teenage girls like they were friends of hers and not high school students. When teachers do this, they are putting themselves in a position to hear things they may not necessarily want to, and once they do hear them, they may have a legal responsibility to pass that information on to a higher authority. In addition, her shocked reaction to the revelation about the young woman's sexual activity, while understandable, was unprofessional. Obviously, this is an extreme case, and being a first-year teacher, Amy was clearly unprepared to hear something so shocking. The best advice to give a new teacher is this: Remember that students and teachers are not equals and try not to put yourself in a position like the one Amy found herself in.

Case Three

The beauty of being a new teacher is that while you may lack experience, you possess something the veteran may not have: a fresh perspective. Chris, who felt that he had seen it all in his ten years of experience, clearly had not. He was operating from the mind-set of the "experienced" teacher and when his tried-and-true strategies did not have an impact, he simply did not know what to do. Had he not gotten and listened to that much-needed wake-up call from his colleague, the rest of his time with those students could have been miserable, and unnecessarily so.

Just as the new teacher has to learn to adjust his or her thinking when transitioning from the chair in front of the teacher's desk to the one behind it, so does the veteran teacher have to take a step back now and then to examine just how and why they teach the way they do. Don't allow yourself to get caught up in a routine that seems to work yet does not allow for change, something teachers should always be engaged in.

FINAL TIPS FOR UNDERSTANDING YOUR STUDENTS

Making the transition from college student, stockbroker, or empty nester to schoolteacher can be a difficult one. No new teacher wants to turn into that jerk of a teacher we all had when we were growing up, and the fact is you don't have to. Just remember that you are a teacher now, not a student. That phase of your life is over and now belongs to the kids sitting in front of you, so let them enjoy it while you enjoy the new phase of life in front of you.

2

ONLY 175 DAYS TO GO . . . HOW TO SURVIVE THE FIRST WEEK OF SCHOOL

When asked about their experiences in school, most people would probably say that they couldn't wait until they came to an end. Looking back, they remember wonderful things like not fitting in, not getting their dream guy or girl, getting bossed around by teachers, and having to do lots of homework. Well, guess what: As a new teacher, you get to look forward to joyous things like not fitting in, not getting to teach your dream class, getting bossed around by administrators, and yes, lots and lots of homework. Caught between wanting to be taken seriously and dreams of popularity, you will make plenty of mistakes during those early September days, some of which may lead to discipline disasters and, if you're not careful, disappointed administrators.

There really is nothing like the first day of school as a new teacher to conjure up all of those painful repressed childhood memories. Even as an adult, the new teacher may find him- or herself desperate over what to wear, panicking over not having anyone to eat lunch with, having nightmares of showing up naked, and obsessing over whether he or she will be good enough to fit in at the new school. Ever visit a school you attended as a child and wonder why many of the same old dinosaurs were still working there? That's probably because they didn't want to be "new" somewhere all over again.

It has been said before and boy, is it true: First impressions count. Your illustrious authors once had the pleasure of working with a "change-of-career" teacher who had disaster written all over him the day he walked in the door. Which, actually, was the second day of school. Don't get us wrong, there is nothing wrong with the change-of-career teacher, but some seem to leave their previous jobs for what they perceive to be the "easy" teacher life, and we all know how accurate that is.

The teacher this gentleman replaced had quit at the last minute, leading the administration to dust off the résumés that remained from the hiring done that summer. He, not surprisingly, was available. Much later in the year, after this teacher was long gone, a colleague of ours asked the assistant superintendent why they chose to hire him. His response? "It was September. He had a pulse."

It's not that he was not a nice man. He simply made some extremely poor decisions about making that first impression. It turned out that we happened to have a number of students in common, and we could tell right away that something major had happened on his first day. His students couldn't wait to tell the tale to anyone that would listen after they left his class. They were all fired up about the new teacher who wrote a song in order to introduce himself. In the spirit of "breaking the ice," he suggested the students do the same.

Obviously, there are plenty of dynamic teachers out there who could actually pull something like that off. He was not one of them. We knew he was in trouble when his students came out of his room wanting to know what a bunion was. When asked why, the student said that, during his introductory song, the new teacher sang about having them. But wait, that's not all. Another piece of information he included was that his college nickname was "the Meatball." This was a move he lived to regret during ethnic foods week in the cafeteria. On the plus side, the cafeteria staff was pleased by the record sales they experienced on Italian Day. Unfortunately, none of those meatballs made it into the students' stomachs. Instead, they ended up stuck to the new teacher's blackboard and desk.

The sad part about this story is that the students were certainly wrong in their behavior. While they should have been the only ones punished, and they indeed faced consequences, the new teacher eventually had to leave because he was never able to regain control. Would things have been different if he had opted against the meatball/bunion song? Perhaps. However, kids have wonderful memories and whatever impression they make of you on the first day, for better or for worse, may in fact be yours for the year.

Making a good first impression in the classroom is only half of what you will need to do as you are getting started, for not only do you have a sea of students to get to know, there are also your colleagues and your bosses. In our years of teaching we have seen a handful of teachers who claim not to care what the rest of the faculty or the administration thinks about them. While it certainly does not make them bad teachers, we don't recommend that attitude. Once you settle into a school you will find that your fellow teachers will become some of your best friends. Let's face it, who else would believe the bunion/meatball story unless they, too, witnessed the backlash firsthand?

No matter what anyone says, as a new teacher (and maybe even as a veteran) you *will* be nervous during the first few days, maybe even weeks. It's to be expected. Look at it this way: If you make it to Halloween, you're probably doing a pretty good job. Until then, just be yourself, think things through carefully, ask for help, and try to have a little fun while you're at it.

COMMON MISTAKES MADE BY NEW TEACHERS DURING THE FIRST FEW DAYS WITH ADULTS

Not Paying Enough Attention at Those First Few Meetings. We know, aside from the free doughnuts, teacher meetings are *so* boring. And it's so easy to fall asleep in an auditorium. However, you may need to know some of the stuff that is discussed, and you should concentrate on burning the faces of the speakers into your brain because they are probably some pretty important folks. You will be hearing from the likes of your superintendent or headmaster, your building principal, as well as your union or faculty representatives, and keep an eye out for the head custodian, who will more than likely have to get up on stage to tell someone to move an illegally parked car (hopefully not yours). You should know all of these people by name and face because they are either in charge of you or they are people you will need things from in the near future.

Talking Too Much While the Head Honchos Are Giving Their Speeches. This sounds like common sense, but you'd be surprised. Being new, you don't want to seem rude or even uncool to anyone, so if the person next to you keeps making snide remarks about this being the same crap they hear every year, it will be tempting to join in on the laughs. However, we all know that this type of behavior is rude and childish and will be the exact thing that will drive you crazy when the students begin doing it to you when classes start. Between the two of us we have endured countless first-day meetings, and it is commonplace to hear quiet chatter on top of the person addressing the crowd at the time. No one ever seemed to mind this childish behavior; at least until one of the most frightening incidents that we have ever seen occurred.

Shortly after our superintendent was done inspiring us to set forth on the best year yet, the assistant superintendent (generally the scariest person in any district) pulled a young middle school teacher aside. He asked her to see him at his office later that day.

Upon her arrival, he ripped her apart for chatting to her colleague for the duration of the speech. Rumors of this incident spread quickly throughout all of the buildings. While many of us thought it was a bit of an urban legend, we (and about thirty or forty of her sympathetic, awestruck colleagues) heard about it firsthand at our local watering hole. While the event may have landed her a number of free beers that afternoon, it also taught the lot of us a hard lesson. It could have been any one of us, and you bet the next year people knew to mind their manners.

Not Asking Enough Questions of Your Veteran Colleagues. Don't try to guess how to use the copier; you will undoubtedly break it and suffer severe unpopularity at the hands of your hundreds of colleagues who have no copies for the first day of school. Don't just assume abandoned staplers, desks, books, file cabinets, pens, and other office supplies are there for the taking. Ask someone where to get those things and get them from the appropriate person. Oh, and most important, that steaming coffee pot from which everyone else in the whole school is drinking is probably not for just anyone to drink from. Most likely, there is a "coffee club" that you put money into, and then and only then are you granted access. Trust us, nothing will get you shunned faster than messing with other people's coffee.

COMMON MISTAKES MADE BY NEW TEACHERS DURING THE FIRST FEW DAYS WITH STUDENTS

Not Being Properly Prepared for a "Short Day." Many schools have abbreviated schedules on the first day to provide students time for things like getting important information during a homeroom, changing a class, and so forth. As a result, some teachers write it off as sort of a free day. They tell the students their name, hand them the supply list, and let them talk for the remainder of the class. This sends a terrible message. Students will immediately form an opinion of you as being extremely laid back. Even if classes are only fifteen minutes long, think of something you can do as a class. Having them write out goals for the year is not only an excellent (and short) assignment, it also shows the kids that you take every day seriously.

Standing in Front of the Class and Reading Rules and Regulations. This also gives the wrong impression. Kids don't want a list of all the things they are not allowed to do. You will look too authoritative and inflexible. While eventually you will have to address acceptable and unacceptable behaviors, it does not have to be the first day. Instead, spend the time doing something to get to know their names and personalities.

Planning Cheesy, Touchy-Feely, Get-to-Know-You-Type Icebreakers. Our fellow English teachers are infamous for these things. While a mild icebreaker activity is appropriate, keep it down-to-earth and educational. Bearing in mind that having the students think you are cool is not something that you should be focused on, you don't want to do anything that will make them think you are a total geek either. So lose all thoughts of having the class form and detangle a "human knot" and forget about having them pass an orange from one classmate to another using only their chins while they try to say the alphabet backward. With the exception of the theater kids, who seem to love these things, the general population doesn't really appreciate them. Of course, you may end up with lots of theater kids, so stock up on plenty of citrus fruit if you are assigned such a class.

CASE STUDIES

Case One: Amy Gets Honored

Not to toot my own proverbial horn, but I must admit that the first day of my first year went flawlessly. It was pretty much downhill from there, but day one could be marked down as a success. I was teaching ninth- and tenth-grade English, and in the spirit of commanding respect and "setting the appropriate tone" I sat each class alphabetically. I told them that we would go over rules and expectations as the week went on, and I started with a light writing and speaking exercise that held their attention and easily filled the shortened class. I have no idea what made me lose my mind the following year.

September 1999 rolled around and, still on a high from actually surviving my first year teaching, I burst through the doors with all the excitement and giddiness of the next homecoming queen. I was thrilled to be reunited with my teacher buddies, I was curiously checking out the new hires, I had purchased at least five pairs of fantastic new shoes, and I was filled with joy when I found out I was teaching honors! This year was going to be a breeze!

I had never had an honors class before, and the previous year I certainly had my share of wise guys. Therefore, I was under the impression that this was going to be a bit of a holiday, starting with day one. I figured that these were smart kids who did their work and had earned the right to a little independence.

This was the plan: They could choose their own seats, and once they were seated they were to choose a partner, interview the partner using the "get-to-know-you" questions we brainstormed at the beginning of class or any questions they felt were appropriate, record the answers, and then "introduce" the partner to the class in the form of an oral presentation. Meanwhile, I was free to traipse around the room, break in my new shoes, and smile warmly upon my new set of eager, honors-level bookworms.

The worst part of the class was that it took me forever to notice just how disastrous that plan was. The fact that it started out well blinded me to what was coming. The brainstorming of questions went well. We discussed the importance of open-ended questions as opposed to those with yes-or-no answers. The kids came up with some great ideas, and then it was time to break into pairs.

Noticing that we had an odd number, I asked that one group work in a set of three as opposed to a pair. This is where the fun began. When I told them to pair up, the class consisted of about six groups of three, four pairs, and three or four kids who did not want to work with anyone. I asked them to reconfigure, and nobody budged. I asked them again, and I heard various forms of "But we're best friends! We haaaaaave to be able to work as a threesome or else how do we decide who has to leave the group?" followed by "Who cares? Why can't we just stay like this? What is the big deal?" along with "Can't I just interview myself?"

I completely panicked, so I told them choosing their own groups was over and that they should all go back to their seats and I was going to pair them up. An uprising that rivaled that of Paris in 1789 followed these instructions. I was Marie Antoinette, they were hungry peasants, and I had just suggested they eat cake. With visions of my head in the guillotine, I walked down the aisles longing for the shoes I wore last year and simply said, "Okay, you two are a pair, you two are a pair, you three are together," and so on. Most of them begrudgingly got down to business, and for a while things were peaceful, at least until I reminded them that they would be giving oral presentations. Most of them took that news in stride. Slowly but surely, however, students began creeping toward my desk:

"Ms. Sutton?"

"Yes?"

"I can't give the oral presentation."

"Why?"

The answers that followed included: "I have a fear of public speaking." "My retainer makes it embarrassing for me to speak in front of the class." "My special education modifications [yes, even in honors classes] excuse me from addressing the class for more than sixty seconds, and the assignment calls for a two-minute speech." "Everyone in this room hates me and will make fun of me." "My partner won't talk to me and it wouldn't be fair for me to be graded on an assignment that I was not in complete control of." "My parents said I don't have to."

I was actually missing my wise guys. The honors curriculum clearly states that public speaking is a major component of the class. I completely understood their fear, but wasn't this something they had to get over regardless of orthodontic apparatuses? Wasn't I a better teacher if I pushed them and did not accept their excuses?

The next day went well, and the class worked hard on their interviews and speeches without my having to refocus them. Things were looking up, but before I knew it, the uprising began. On the day of the speeches, one girl stood up and said, "I would give my oral presentation, but my partner doesn't talk so I guess I'll just take a zero."

I let that one go, and soon after another bomb went off. I called a student's name, and he simply said, "I'd like to pass on my turn."

What? I had no other choice but to move on, and naturally the next person I called wanted to know if he could pass on his turn too. I tried to be as sensitive as possible with my answer:

"Absolutely not."

"But why not? You let him!"

"That doesn't matter."

"It's not fair!"

"No, it's not, but I am sure you have a wonderful speech there and we would not want to deprive the class of your oratory skills."

"Of my what?"

"Just make the speech."

"Fine!"

Thankfully, being that it was the first week, periods were shortened due to special homeroom activities. The bell rang in the middle of the poor kid's speech, but I did not care. In spite of the fact that I put up with an enormous amount of strife my first year, I never wanted a class to end as badly as it did in this first week of my second year.

Case Two: Never Turn Your Back on the (Middle School) Class

Not every teacher begins their career on the first day of school. I have the distinct honor of being one of the people that got his or her "big break" by finishing out the school year when someone was promoted, went on maternity leave, quit, or died. And so it was that I began my teaching career in the very junior high school that I had graduated from way back in 1986. I had substituted there a few times to "get my foot in the door" and because of that, when a position needed to be filled very quickly, I was their man. So here I was, fresh out of college, working in the school of my youth, and being hit on by my old gym teacher. What could go wrong? Well, a lot.

Bear in mind, with the exception of some substitute work, which usually involved handing out the assignment that was left for me, collecting it at the end of the period, and making sure the kids stayed in the room in the interim, I had virtually no teaching experience, save my student teaching experience, which conveniently took place in the friendly confines of the high school I graduated from. This fact must be made clear in order for you to comprehend how it would be possible to make so many mistakes on my very first day, mistakes that could have resulted in accusations leveled at me for assaulting a student, wearing an offensive article of clothing, terrifying a group of honors students, and insulting my principal. While I may be exaggerating just a bit here, you will soon see why I chose to present these facts to you in this manner.

The day started normally enough. I arrived bright and early wearing a pair of dark slacks my mother had given to me, armed with the briefcase my future wife bought me for Christmas (which now supports one of the broken legs that holds up my mattress), and all kinds of enthusiasm. I had been given my program the day before, which consisted of a seventh-grade honors English class (about as honorable as twelve-year-olds can be, I suppose), an eighth-grade "regular" English class, and three sections of something called Home and Careers. Oddly enough, no one bothered to explain to me exactly what one did in Home and Careers. No problem, I thought. I'll just ask the kids! I'm sure they'll be glad to help. But that wasn't until the end of the day. First, I had to get through my first class with the seventh graders.

This would be easy, I told myself. Not only had I substituted for this particular group of kids before, I had also been in to introduce myself as their new teacher a day earlier, so the transfer of power would be seamless. I got to my room early and made sure all the day's work was on the board. I wanted everything to be perfect. Suddenly, the first bell rang and I bolted to the door, now overcome with nerves. First impression, I told myself, first impression.

I smiled warmly at each child that entered the room. Four minutes later, the late bell rang and it was show time. I asked the children to take out their copies of *The Secret Garden* (I had prepared for class, of course) when three kids entered the room. They were in pretty high spirits for a bunch of kids who were strolling into class late, I might add. Taking advantage of the new guy on his first day, huh? Well, I could play bad cop with the best of them. I immediately engaged my "mean" persona: "Who do you guys think you are, coming in late? Where's your late pass?"

The smallest of them answered me in a voice so tiny that to this day I feel guilty about this incident: "We don't have one."

First impression, Chris, show 'em who's boss: "Why not?"

Another terrified little child chimed in: "We had to pick up our tickets for the Spring Concert."

"I didn't ask where you were! I asked why you don't have a pass!"

The third and weakest little runt of the litter finally found the courage to speak: "But they said that the tickets would be our pass."

Oh, now I had heard everything. "That's ridiculous! Now go back to wherever you were and get a late pass!"

They scurried out like scared rabbits, and I returned my attention to the class, my "good cop" smile back on my face: "Now where were we? Ah! *The Secret Garden*! Who would like to read from the beginning of chapter three?"

They stared at me like I had just beaten up Santa Claus and molested the Easter Bunny. Miraculously, we got through the period without anyone bursting into tears.

With that nightmare over (or so I thought), I moved on to my eighth-grade class, which consisted of the kids working as quietly as church mice for the teacher that taught a vocabulary mini-lesson to them every day, only to have everything descend into chaos the second he left the room when I tried to teach my lesson. After that I had a free period in which I smiled politely and said "fine" whenever any of the other teachers present asked me how it was going so far, all the time thinking, "What the hell have I gotten myself into?" After that I had lunch duty, where I watched the kids fuel up so they had enough strength to terrorize for four more periods.

As I walked around the cafeteria and pretended not to hear the kids making fun of my thinning hair, I saw a young male student running through the cafeteria at what could only be described as an unsafe speed. He ignored another teacher's orders to stop, and I saw my chance to become "superteacher." As he approached me, I stuck out my arm and tried to emulate what professional wrestlers like to call the "clothesline" move. To our mutual surprise, the move worked, catching the boy in the midsection. Proudly, I escorted him up to the dean's office for all in the cafeteria to see. Sorry, pal. Not on my watch. We didn't do things like that when I went to school here.

After dropping the boy off with the stunned dean of students, I started back to the cafeteria, only to be intercepted by an assistant principal, who asked me to come into her office. Probably wants to thank me, I thought. Yeah, sure.

"Please sit down, Mr. Purr." I did with pleasure. "Mr. Purr, what possessed you to throw a wrestling move on that boy and humiliate him by dragging him up to the dean's office in front of the entire seventh grade?"

I must admit, I hadn't seen this coming! "Well, he was running and . . . "

"Did you tell him to stop?"

"Well, no, but another teacher . . . "

"Mr. Purr, unless you are looking forward to having a lawsuit leveled against you, I would refrain from putting your hands on any more students unless it is absolutely necessary. Do I make myself clear?"

"Yes, of course. It will never happen again." Thank God that was over. I made a movement like I was going to get up and leave, another blunder.

"There's one more thing, Mr. Purr, if you don't mind." This wasn't going to be good.

"Yes?"

"Mr. Purr, what happened during your first-period class?

"Nothing. Why?"

"Because I had three honors students in here crying their eyes out this morning because you kicked them out of class!"

I was really, really glad I had taken the job here. "What? Kicked? They came to class late without a pass!"

She apparently didn't care for my explanation. Instead, she responded with a line so stupid yet true that I will never forget it: "Mr. Purr, these aren't bad kids! They're bubbies!"

I left the office and headed for three periods of Home and Careers, the class I assumed the kids would tell me how to teach. And what a bunch of "bubbies" they were. As I quickly found out, Home and Careers, at least in this school, was the dumping ground for kids that didn't quite cut it in art or music. Needless to say, the kids were of no help. Thankfully, I found a stack of workbooks in a closet that might have indirectly been related to some type of home or career and handed them out. I decided on an assignment and turned to the blackboard to write it down when the pandemonium in the room was replaced by a quiet snickering. I turned to look at the class and asked what was so funny. One boy, clearly not shy, responded, "Hey, Mr. Purr, where'd you get them black pants?"

I tried to see if I had a stain on my rear but could not. "Why?"

The boy responded by standing up, turning to the class, and yelling: "Mr. Purr got his Dickies on!"

Now, for those of you who don't know, Dickies are a high-quality brand of work clothes. While they are mostly associated with outdoor work, they do make a wonderful pair of black slacks, ideal for any office-type setting. The only drawback to them, in my opinion, would be the massive orange-and-blue patch with the word *Dickies* emblazoned on the back. While this may not present much of a problem in a blue-collar type of setting, you might want to reconsider wearing them in a class full of seventh-grade kids that can't cut it in art or music. Naturally, I was greeted to a chorus of "Dickies! Dickies!" for the rest of that day, a day that refused to end.

It turned out that my other free period was at the end of the day, which I welcomed greatly after the experiences I had just gone through. After I took a few moments to collect myself, I decided that I might as well go home. I decided to walk through the main office and say good-bye to the secretarial staff who had been so instrumental in my getting hired. As I said my farewells, I bumped into the school principal. Naturally, I offered him a hearty "See you tomorrow!"

Stunned, he just watched me walk toward the exit for a few moments before saying, "Where do you think you're going?"

I froze in place. What the hell did I do now? "Home. I'm off eighth period."

He glared at me, with a look of disgust on his face, adding: "The day ends at three o'clock. Go do some hall duty on the second floor."

Humiliated, I completed my first day on the job by marching up to the second floor to begin the hall duty assignment that would replace my free period for the rest of my (brief) stay there.

ADMINISTRATIVE ANALYSIS

Case One

Amy's first mistake was forgetting that, regardless of skill level, younger students benefit from a structured lesson. I do agree that honors classes allow for more freedom, but not until later in the year and preferably under the watchful eye of a more experienced teacher. This point will be repeated often, but having a good reputation in the school enables you to be a little more experimental because students know that your class needs to be taken seriously. Even an excellent, experienced teacher who happens to be new to the building has to be patient and wait until his or her classroom tone is established before abandoning a sense of structure in favor of a more loosely instructed lesson.

Being that it was the first day and Amy had no idea what the students in the class were going to be like, she should have most definitely assigned them their seats, which she could later rearrange when she got to know the students better.

Amy's next mistake was not the actual assignment, which was a perfect opening to an honors English class, it was allowing students to choose their partners. She had no idea if there was a student in the room who would never convince another to work with him or her, or a clique of students who would monopolize the class if allowed to work together. Assigning pairs saves the so-called unpopular students from the embarrassment of not being chosen, and it saves the instructor from being overwhelmed by the more "friendly" pairs.

In addition, assigning pairs forces students to meet and bond with kids they normally would not have interacted with, which is always good for high school students. Later in the year, when the class is familiar to the teacher, having students choose their own pairs and groups would be fine if the class can function appropriately when given that freedom.

The most difficult aspect of Amy's lesson was the students' trying to get out of making the speeches. This is always a tough situation, and although teachers often get criticized for acting inconsistently, certain situations need to be evaluated on a case-by-case basis. If a student has an individual education plan (IEP) that excuses him or her from speaking aloud to the class, there is nothing the teacher can do. Occasionally, you may have a student that is sensitive about having a speech impediment. In this case, the student can be given the option to deliver the oral report privately, possibly after school in front of you and perhaps a trusted friend of the student. Some students are simply terrified of speaking in public, and gently encouraging them to go first in order to get it over with is often a good solution.

The important thing for these situations, however, is to address all of your students' special concerns privately. You will find that the kids with legitimate problems will actually come see you, and you may want to consult those students' past teachers to see how they handled the situation. The kids who simply don't feel like doing the assignment probably won't bother coming to see you at all, and they will either begrudgingly do the assignment or come to class unprepared. If they choose the latter, you have a leg to stand on because you had offered them the option of discussing the problem after school.

Case Two

Chris found himself in trouble on his first day by trying to be too strict. Many teachers think they have to play "bad cop" when they start teaching in order to establish classroom control. While it is important to be firm with your students, it doesn't mean you have to act like a drill sergeant. Telling his kids to "go get a late pass" was a bad idea. Instead, he should have allowed the students in and spoken to them at the end of class to try and get to the bottom of the situation. Sending kids out that come late to class is a bad idea in general, as it encourages them to take the slow boat back to wherever they were and they end up missing even more class time. Deal with it later, and make sure that you do; otherwise you can guarantee that those kids will be late every day.

Be very, very careful when you choose to put your hands on a child. There is a time and a place for it (see chapter 7, on violence, for more), but unless someone is in imminent danger of being harmed, try to refrain from "clotheslining" every student that you catch running in the hall, because there will be many of them. Instead, follow the lead of the previous teacher that told the boy to stop and do the same. If the student refuses, wait until he or she tires and then deal with him or her privately. Parading the student through the cafeteria will only add to any feelings of defiance the child may already have.

Chris not being prepared for his Home and Careers class was absolutely inexcusable. He should have asked for help with the course from fellow colleagues, an administrator, or anyone else he could get his hands on. As you will read elsewhere in this book (see chapter 3), being prepared is essential if you want to succeed in teaching. If he was unable to learn anything about the class from his colleagues beforehand, then he should have come up with something himself the night before. Chris wanted to make a good first impression and instead he made a terrible one. And as far as his "Dickies" are concerned, twelve-year-olds are going to behave like twelve-year-olds, so dress accordingly.

FINAL TIPS FOR THE FIRST FEW DAYS

No matter what subject you teach, you may want to try an activity on the first day that helps you get to know your students' names and allows them limited, structured time to catch up with each other. Having students interview each other like Amy did (well, not *exactly* like Amy did) can work if done correctly. It is important, however, to get as many students speaking out loud as possible.

One of the absolute best teachers we know who teaches some of the most difficult kids in the school does a first-day activity where she has students brainstorm the characteristics of a good teacher. They write them down on big rolls of paper, and they are posted on the walls all year. She has them do the same for the characteristics of a good student. It doesn't take long; it holds their attention; it gets them talking, thinking, and moving around; and it is something to refer to as the year goes on.

Forget the rule about not smiling until after December. If you are in a comfortable enough situation and you feel a smile coming on, go with it! Being seen as a happy, approachable person will not result in the eruption of chaos. If a class is structured so that disaster will occur, it will occur whether you are smiling or frowning. Trust us, you will have more success with the kids if they perceive that you are happy to be there.

Be aware that the administration loves to pop in on classes during the first few days of the school year. First, they have the time because all hell hasn't broken loose yet, and they don't have a mile-long line of kids snaking out of their office doors. Second, they like to get a visual idea of where their teachers are located that year, in case they need them. Finally, they are curious to see what is going on in each room. You can tell a lot by the way a teacher structures the first day, and principals and headmasters are looking to see teachers interacting with students. Again, standing there and reading a list of rules is not going to make a good impression on your boss or students.

Get to know your colleagues. If someone invites you out to wherever it is they go to unwind, go with them. This is an excellent way to not only get some much deserved downtime, but it will also allow you to connect with your colleagues, whom you may be working with for a very long time. If there is not much after-school fraternization where you work, try starting it up yourself. Talk your fellow rookies into getting together to talk about the highs and lows of your first week. Meeting for a drink and a joke can be very therapeutic. And who knows? You might even inspire some of the old-timers to join you.

The old saying is true: The hardest part is getting started. When you are stressed out during your first days as a teacher, try to remember that all those veterans around you were in the same boat as you at one point. Their prowess in the classroom did not develop overnight, and it probably won't for you either. Don't let that discourage you. Before you know it, you will be just as comfortable as the old-timers once you have some experience under your belt. In fact, you might just have some of them asking you for advice once you start to shine.

3

HAVE YOU SEEN MY GRADE BOOK? GETTING ORGANIZED SO YOU NEVER HAVE TO ASK THAT DREADED QUESTION

If we both had to name our greatest weakness as teachers, it would definitely be organization. We have lost grade books, videos, library books (God help you if you ever get on the bad side of your school librarian), and, worst of all, student work. One of us has had our desk called a pigsty, and that was from a close friend and colleague. Can a teacher sink any lower? Well, yes. Your other illustrious author once lost an entire book bag that contained stacks and stacks of student work. The unnamed person ended up lying to the classes, resorting to that most sophomoric of prevarications, "My car was broken into!"

Who knew there was a black market for student essays that haven't been graded yet? That is what a lack of organization can do to you. It can turn you into a liar. It can turn you into a crazed lunatic who rifles through every desk in the building in search of the grade book that is safely nestled on the desk in the copy room where it was left at 7:15 in the morning when you were making the copies you should have made the day before. Being unorganized can really catch up with you. Take it from two recovering airheads.

We have a colleague who is, shall we say, as retentive as he is charming. He has every assignment he has ever written placed beautifully in plastic pockets and then bound into a three-ring binder, all in the exact order in which he uses them. If that's not enough, he tapes a copy of each daily handout in his plan book (*plan book* really doesn't do it justice; it's more like an illuminated manuscript) so that he can flip back to it to see how he did things the year before. Maintaining these systems takes quite a bit of time out of his days, and when questioned on where he finds the time to do all that, he answered, "I don't have the time not to." Excellent point.

Think of all the time he saves each year not digging through file cabinets, cardboard boxes, and computer files searching for his assignments and exams. And no, he's not one of those people who teaches from the same yellowed notes each year. Not only does he constantly change things around to keep his lessons fresh and interesting, he saves an enormous amount of planning time by looking in the previous year's plan book. Unfortunately, not all teachers are like that. So unless you think you might enjoy reinventing the wheel every year, take note to work on your organizational skills.

COMMON ORGANIZATION MISTAKES MADE BY NEW TEACHERS

Not Having a Place to Keep Your "Stuff." Being the new kid in town, be prepared to discover that your new colleagues have more than likely snatched up any real estate the teacher you are replacing left behind. It's your job to see to it that you have a place to land every morning. Searching high and low for everything from your coffee mug to your classroom keys takes time out of your day and years off your life. The stress of missing important items is enormous; however, it is one of the few anxiety triggers associated with teaching that can be prevented by finding a "spot" of your own to keep your most prized possessions. With enrollment in schools going through the roof (sometimes literally) teachers are constantly losing the space they used for grading papers, calling parents, and counting the seconds until their lunch period ends. Nevertheless, find a place and grab on. An area on a bookshelf is fine, as long as it's yours.

Losing a Student's Work. It happens to everyone except the divinely organized. Most teachers do not realize they lost a kid's paper until they go to mark it down in the grade book. The best way to prevent this is to collect student work individually as opposed to having them pass it up to you. Then, if a student does not hand in an assignment, you have it marked down and there are no questions later. In addition, the kids may try a little harder to get it done now that they know they will be getting a personal visit from you every day.

Not Dealing with Student Absences Properly. With class sizes being what they are today, it's easy for a kid that has been absent to get lost in the shuffle. Be careful you don't shuffle your way into some trouble by neglecting to have assignments available if and when you are asked for them. There is nothing worse than being in the middle of teaching a lesson when there is a knock on your door from a monitor looking for that make-up work you were supposed to send down for a child who had her wisdom teeth pulled five days ago. Actually, what would be worse would be if the child's mother and father (or nanny, or legal guardian, or legal counsel, you just never know) were sitting down in the office annoying all of the secretaries and pestering the guidance counselors.

Don't put yourself in a position where you must stop what you are doing and dig all around your desk looking for several days' worth of assignments, spare textbooks, and the ever-elusive pen to write the caring little note about feeling better and coming back soon. What you should do is start a folder containing the missed work for that child as soon as you realize the child is out. When the knock comes, you won't even have to break eye contact with your class; you simply grab the folder and pass it on without missing a beat.

Failing to Prepare for Your Own Absence. This mistake is a bad one because it can potentially inconvenience a lot of people. First and foremost, we have the secretaries. Any honest principal will tell you that it is the secretaries that really run a school building, and you will want to do everything humanly possible to stay in their good graces. Then of course, there is the substitute, who will have to resort to old Vaudeville routines in order to entertain your classes because you didn't leave an assignment. Last, but not least, there are your kind-hearted colleagues that will try to find something for the substitute to use so they don't have to listen to "Hello, my baby, hello, my darling" all day long from next door. They have a hard enough time preparing for their own classes. Don't burden them with having to prepare for yours as well.

Make sure you have assignments ready for all of your classes and make sure they are where they are supposed to be. Most of the time it's with the aforementioned secretaries. Also make sure to run off plenty of copies, and throw in an attendance sheet as well. Better yet, don't be absent. It just creates double the work for you when you come back.

Running Short of Material. You were up all night preparing the greatest lesson ever devised. This one is going to knock 'em dead. You might even try to get it published. You think of becoming an adjunct at the local community college. You get to class five minutes earlier than usual because you can't contain your excitement. The class comes in and they eat it up. Educational Nirvana. One problem: You're done in fifteen minutes. What looks like a forty-minute presentation on paper quite often turns out this way. Don't fall into the trap of only planning for the following day. The "one day at a time" approach is great if you're in recovery, but not in the classroom. Plan as far ahead as you can, and always assume you are going to run short. This way you can start on the next day's material and nobody's the wiser. Good old bell-to-bell instruction.

CASE STUDIES

Case One: The Case of the Missing Mockingbird

It was the first major assignment I ever gave as an English teacher. It was early October, and the students were writing a short paper on *To Kill a Mockingbird*. It was the end of the class, and time was running out so instead of going around and collecting the papers individually, I had the students pass them up the rows. The papers were supposed to be five pages, and they were due the same week as progress reports.

Progress reports are one of those annoying things that should not, but do, take forever to complete. Before I could even begin to calculate a possible grade range I had several other small but time-consuming tasks to complete. I had to catch up on grading make-up work, I had to examine and consider each student's class participation, I had to calculate absences, and I also needed to catch up on the grading of a few homework assignments. I grossly underestimated the time this would take, and the *Mockingbird* papers, their major grade for the quarter, kept getting more and more buried. Luckily, I did not need to grade them before the progress reports were due. However, neglecting them would soon prove to be a big mistake.

With the daunting task of progress reporting behind me, I settled in one Sunday afternoon to grade the enormous pile of *To Kill a Mockingbird* papers. Four hours later, my head still spinning with thoughts of Boo Radley, chifforobes, and damn ham, I eagerly went to record the grades of the completed papers.

As I was double-checking to make sure the appropriate grade was placed in the appropriate student's column in my grade book, I noticed that there were three students who had no grade next to their names, and no indication that they had failed to turn in the paper in class on the due date. I was a little confused (and very naive) because the students *know* that if they approach me after class to ask for help or to explain why the paper is late, I'll give them extra time with little or no penalty. My theory was, and still is, that the main goal was that they have the learning experience of writing the paper. If something keeps them from sticking to the due date, that's something that can be worked around.

Later that night, after making it through another pile of papers, I decided to look through each folder to make sure the three missing papers weren't mixed up in another stack. Still no luck, so I decided to speak with the students the next day.

Mondays are always tough, and this one started out by being extra difficult. I handed the graded papers back to the students, and two of the students who did not receive one remained silent. I quietly asked them to see me after class to discuss the fact that they did not hand anything in, and they sheepishly agreed. As I approached the third student, who was notorious for missing assignments, things took a dramatic turn:

"Ms. Sutton!"

"Yes, Robbie?"

"Are there any more papers?"

"No, I'm afraid that's it."

"But I didn't get one!"

"I know you didn't, so why don't you see me after class and we'll see what we can do?"

"But I'll be late for math!"

"I'll write you a pass. Everyone, put your papers away. Moving on to . . . "

"But Ms. Sutton! I want to know my grade!"

"We'll talk later."

"But I gave you one and everyone else got theirs back now and I want to know my grade!"

"Robbie. See. Me. After. Class."

"Aaaaall right!"

The class moved on, but my students were certainly intrigued by the dramatic events that proceeded to unfold. They weren't really settled, and to be honest neither was I. When the bell rang, three students surrounded my desk. For the first two, I did not want to give them a chance to "pull a Robbie" so I told them that I needed the paper by Thursday, and if they needed help to see me after school. I quickly dismissed them.

By this point, Robbie was literally bouncing off the walls. Shuffling from side to side and pulling at his Derek Jeter T-shirt, he couldn't wait to stop this grave injustice that he had suffered. He declared with great passion that he had stayed up all night, spent hours in the library, and even given up tickets to a Yankee game where he would have witnessed them clinch the pennant. It was the third lie that convinced me that there was no possibility in the entire universe that he was telling the truth. No self-respecting kid in my school district would ever admit to a sin like missing a Yankee game!

I told him that I did not receive a paper from him, and he insisted that I did. I told him I looked through all of my things hundreds of times in case the mistake was on my end, but my search was unsuccessful. He still would not give in. Finally, I told him that he had two choices: If he had really done the paper, he could go home, print up a new copy, turn it in the next day without receiving a penalty, and I would have it graded by the end of the day for him.

He answered the way I expected him to by telling me that he did not save the paper on his computer. I told him I had a feeling that that would be the case, and I was willing to accept the paper on Thursday with a penalty. It was then that he broke into a tirade about the injustice of it all. I was not fair, this school was not fair, the middle school was not fair, and come to think of it, his preschool was not fair. He carried on about all teachers hating him, never believing him, and always taking other students at their word and not him. I finally dismissed him, and told him I had to think about how to handle this.

I really did not know what to do. I was *absolutely positive* that he was lying. I didn't think my luck could possibly be so bad that the one paper I lost turned out to be that of a kid who never handed anything in anyway. I decided to call his mother during my first break:

"Hello, Robbie's mom?"

"Yes, speaking."

"This is Ms. Sutton, Robbie's English teacher."

"Hello."

"I was wondering if you could help me with a little problem . . . "

"Robbie called me from his cell phone about an hour ago and told me about the little problem."

"Oh, well, that's good. I was wondering if you could encourage him to write the paper. The late penalty really is quite minimal, and it is a major grade for the quarter."

"Why would I encourage him to write a paper he already wrote?"

"Well, Robbie's mom, I really don't think he wrote it. You see, I offered to accept the paper with no penalty if he would just print a new one out and hand it in first thing tomorrow. However, he claims he did not save it, which seems a bit odd."

"Well, you know, Robbie struggles, and with all of the pressure on him to get this assignment done, I am not surprised he over-looked saving it."

"I understand that, but I don't see any other options. I need to have a paper in order to give him a grade."

"Yes, but he says you lost it."

"I don't believe that is the case, especially since Robbie does have a bit of a tendency to forget to hand in assignments."

"Robbie told me that you don't like him."

"I have no problem with Robbie. I just need him to complete the assignment."

"Well, I can't see making him rewrite a paper he already wrote."

"Well, Robbie's mom, the only other option is a zero."

"A zero on a paper he wrote?"

"Well, what do you suggest I give him?"

"I suggest it is automatically a hundred being that it is your fault that there is no paper to grade."

"Robbie's mom?"

"Yes?"

"The bell is ringing. I'll have to get back to you."

Case Two: Chris Goes Down for the Count

Restaurants have the Health Department, the police have Internal Affairs, and New York City teachers have the surprise observation from the school principal. There are fewer things more frightening to an untenured teacher, I assure you. This is the tale of woe that I will spin for you now. And, as you can probably guess, things did not go as well as I would have liked. In fact, I would have done better with an actual health inspector doing the observation. The moment I saw him enter the room, one thought exploded in my mind: By the time this inspection was over, there would be more than dust on his gloves.

Problem number one was my plan for that day: To administer a test on Robert Lipsyte's boxing novel *The Contender*. Now some of you out there might be thinking, "Hey, that's an easy one! How can you screw that up?" Quite easily, I assure you. I tried to fend him off: "Oh, hi! Are you here for an observation?"

He responded with a smile, the smile of a man that knows he has just caught someone off guard: "Yes, Mr. Purr. Is now a bad time?"

Oh yeah, like I'm going to say, "Yes sir, this is an awful time. I'm horribly unprepared. Please come back tomorrow. I promise I'll stay up all night and write up a lesson plan that will knock your socks off." The agony continued: "Well, I'm giving a test today. There really won't be much to observe."

Here is something everyone reading this book needs to understand. Just like celebrities, cops, and astronauts are regular people too, so are high school principals. I'm sure he had a million other things to do that day and rescheduling me is not something he would have liked to add to that list. Also, he probably figured he could get my observation out of the way without having to think very much. Apparently he wasn't into having his socks knocked off: "That's okay. I'll just evaluate the test."

It was at this moment that my skin really began to crawl. For you see, while I had every confidence in my proctoring skills, there are some things about the test I haven't shared with you yet that left me a little less than self-assured. Chief among these facts was that the test was copied from a commercially produced study guide, so the principal would really not be evaluating work of mine, but the good people at Pearson Education. Perhaps now you can understand some of my terror. Is there anything wrong with using a commercially produced test, you ask? Well, up until that point, it was certainly okay with *me*, but what you need to be concerned about is the attitude of someone in a position to evaluate you. Judging by the look on his face, I don't think he was very impressed. At least the initial shock of him seeing "Copyright Pearson Education" emblazoned all over the exam was over. But don't worry: The real trouble was just about to start.

I handed the exams to the first child in each row so they could then pass the rest back, watching the principal from the corner of my eye the whole time. Only the top of his bald head was visible as he scribbled what were surely less-than-favorable notes about my brilliant teaching. And as I reached the next-to-last row, my humiliation became even greater. I went to hand the waiting student a stack of exams, only to discover that I had run out of copies that were stapled together. I remember mumbling some sort of apology to the students about not having enough stapled copies and that I would come around with my stapler and rectify that mistake at their seats as they were taking the exam.

Once again I got to look at the bald area as the principal's head shot down to document the work of this most masterful of teachers. I suppose one good thing that came out of this was the fact that he didn't know why I didn't have enough stapled copies: I had used the same exam the period before and walked around and stapled it at their seats. The problem was that it was a smaller class and I hadn't bothered to staple extras while they were taking it. It was textbook laziness in action. Well, that's it, isn't it? I mean, what else could possibly go wrong? Read on, ye of little faith.

At the very least, he got to see some first-class proctoring that day. I was on those kids like white on rice, like a fly on . . . well, you get the idea. There would not be any cheating on that test I did not have a hand in creating, thank you very much. The period was almost over. I was going to make it! Most of the kids were either finished or on the verge of finishing as the bell rang. The principal got up out of his chair and marched up to the front of the room. A few more steps and he would be gone. Naturally, it didn't go down that way. Instead, he turned to a boy seated in the front and said: "Who's Jackie Collins?"

I'll never forget that boy. He was one of those kids that could be hilariously funny at one moment and the next he'd cough up something nasty and spit it on the floor. He looked up at the man and said, with just a dash of Bill and Ted: "Isn't she, like, a writer?"

The principal, having been robbed of this final victory, nodded.

The second that man was out of the room, I scanned the test for the reference. I found it on the last page. The question asked something about the type of books the main character's mother would read, and Jackie Collins was one of the incorrect choices. This is a fact I would have known, had I in fact even looked at the test before I administered it. Oh, didn't I mention that? Yeah, not even once.

ADMINISTRATIVE ANALYSIS

Case One

Amy's mistake was obvious. You should *always* write down who has and has not handed in assignments, and you should also write down who was absent. You may notice that some students have a pattern of being absent on days when large assignments are due in your class or your colleagues' classes, and you may want to have a policy that the paper should be e-mailed to you by the beginning of the school day if the student is going to be absent for only one day or for only part of the day. These students who are too ill to make it to school in time to hand in the paper for you may be miraculously cured in time for their lacrosse game, student council car wash, or hand-bell choir practice later on.

While the above can be chalked up to a lesson learned the hard way, Amy's true dilemma is how to handle Robbie. He needs a grade, but getting him to write the paper, albeit the right thing to do, is not going to happen. It is an ugly truth, but sometimes we must give in to unreasonable parental demands when they are generally innocuous. As an administrator, I would suggest that Amy get an average of all of Robbie's assignments and use that average as his grade for the essay. If the grade is respectable, so be it. If it is not, then Robbie's mom may convince him to write the paper instead. Or she may start the battle all over again. If that happens, the teacher is now in the position to stand firm on her decision because she's already shown her willingness to compromise, which goes a long way in the eyes of an administrator.

Case Two

There are obviously some things about Chris's observation story that demand comment. Let's start with his decision to use a commercially produced test. I don't have a problem with teachers using such things in their classes, as long as they are used properly. Failing to staple them together was the least of Chris's problems. Not having read the test showed very poor judgment on his part. How else would he know if there were questions that dealt with issues from the novel that he hadn't covered in class? If he had planned ahead and not waited for the last minute, that entire uncomfortable scene could have been avoided.

Another thing he could have done had he been a little more forward thinking would have been to retype the test. Administering a test you clearly did not write suggests not only to an administrator that you are lazy, but more important suggests it to your students. Is that the impression you want to give to them? Chris really set himself up for failure through his lack of planning. I suspect (and hope) he learned his lesson and hasn't done anything like that since. While I'm laying blame, I should also comment on the impromptu questioning of the student by the principal. I get the impression that he was hoping to get the wrong answer, and that shows a lack of faith in that child. That was very unprofessional on his part. It appears the sharpest person in the room that day was a teenager, not one of the highly trained professionals.

FINAL TIPS ON ORGANIZATION

We highly suggest emulating our colleague and purchasing and filling the big binder. Keep all lesson plans, with the accompanying handouts, shoved into little plastic pockets. Of course, you'll want to back everything up on a disk. However, if you keep a hard copy of your assignments accessible, you will still be able to copy your work when the computers are down (a weekly event in many places) or when you simply can't get to a computer. In addition, if you are absent and you did not follow our advice about emergency plans, the binder is a place where your disgruntled colleagues can go to find something for your class to do. It takes time to maintain the binder properly, but it is absolutely worth it.

When a student fails to turn in an assignment, write it down. And when giving a test, check to make sure each kid has written his or her name on it and that he or she actually hands it in. Once in a while, a kid will panic on a test and either fail to put his or her name on it or, worse yet, slip it into his or her book bag. In the best-case scenario, in the spirit of mea culpa, you will offer the student a chance to retake it and he or she will quietly comply. In the worst case, the student will throw a fit and tell his or her mom, the principal, and the superintendent how irresponsible you are for losing the test that he or she will swear they scored 100 percent on and you are left wondering how your career hit bottom so rapidly.

Take note of who is absent. Get a folder and stuff it with the assignments for each day the student is absent, and include your e-mail. Have it ready at a moment's notice. The guidance counselors and secretaries will love you!

The administration will probably actually ask you for emergency sub plans. Even so, keep an extra set with a colleague just to be safe. Keep your grade book in the same place at all times, and return it to that place when you are finished using it. Ditto with the car keys and the coffee mug. If possible, keep your things locked up. We love kids, but we know they are capable of pure evil, especially with a substitute teacher in the room. Even the "good ones" are capable of snatching the copies you left for your sub and throwing them in the garbage. Worse yet, the craftier ones may even take the copies for the day, leave the top one, and replace the rest with something pornographic. It's been done before.

Organization is often the most challenging skill for new teachers because it does not always come naturally. Most likely, people who choose to teach have a talent and a desire to work with young people and a passion for their subject. This does not mean you have a passion for filing lesson plans. If you are one of those people who was born organized, you are a step ahead of the rest of us. And, as unorganized people, we know how frustrating it is to share a room with slobs like us and we apologize on behalf of us all. If you can get into good habits during your first few years when making an impression really counts, you may be able to carry these positive practices all the way to retirement.

Ms. Benson decided to take advantage of the fact that most of her students were suspended.

4

BEHAVE YOURSELF! DISCIPLINE AND THE NEW TEACHER

Perhaps the most difficult thing to deal with as a teacher today is the unruly behavior of students, whether it is passive resistance or an obscenity-filled outburst. The days of "spare the rod and spoil the child" have clearly passed, and new teachers find themselves in a political conundrum. Being new to a career, they are held back by fear of seeming too lax and nervousness about being perceived as too strict. In addition, new teachers must also be able to find a balance between their own disciplinary philosophy (if they have one) and the established tone of the building. This task is not an easy one, and it is full of questions with few right answers.

We were once asked to participate in a round of interviews for a new English teacher. We thought it would be an interesting experience and accepted. Interesting does not begin to describe the experience. There were many applicants for the position, and their level of qualifications varied considerably, as did their interview skills. There was one applicant in particular that, to this very day, causes us to stifle a chuckle when the topic of discipline is raised.

She was fresh out of college, with a powerful smile and an even more powerful résumé. She graduated at the top of her class, and her student teaching experience was in one of the best schools in upscale Westchester County, New York. She went on and on about her expertise in the teaching of grammar, her marvelous success using portfolio assessment, and even swore she could make *Ethan Frome* interesting. She seemed like the perfect candidate. It was then that the illustrious administrator chairing the interview went for his trick pitch, the kind Negro League legend Satchel Paige used to call his "Trouble Ball." It would seem to come at you in a straightforward fashion, but at the last minute the bottom would drop out of it and you were left staring into space, expressionless.

A straightforward question on the subject of discipline might be something like, "How would you deal with a class of diverse students that chronically misbehave?" That wasn't his style. Instead, he asked, point-blank, "How do you deal with a kid you don't like?"

Oh, the humanity. It was the Hindenburg all over again.

Her face turned beet red. She looked to the panel of teachers for help, yet there was none to give. How would she adapt her rehearsed answer to this one? A kid I don't like? Why, I could never dislike a student! At least that's what she should have said. But she didn't. Instead, to the amazement of the onlookers below, she went up in flames, managing to stammer out something like, "Well, I guess I'd make him sit in the back of the room or stand in the hall until he quieted down." What? Send him to the back of the room? What were they teaching the kids in college these days? You *never* say anything like that on an interview. Needless to say, the interview ended shortly thereafter and she did not get the job, regardless of the fact that she may have, without realizing it, been absolutely right.

Now, before you start writing your hate mail, let us clarify a few things. The question the former applicant was asked may have been a little unfair. After all, she was a new teacher and hadn't had the opportunity to learn to dislike her students yet. However, for a seasoned teacher, I feel the question is absolutely valid, as it is a foregone conclusion that there will be students that drive teachers crazy, that will push them to their limits, and it is for these students that using the term "dislike" is being polite. Filling out a behavior referral in triplicate, despite what some experts may say, is not necessarily the best way to deal with every infraction. Sometimes, having the kid count the tiles in the hallway is just fine, and it saves you, the student, and an already overwhelmed administrator unnecessary grief.

How *does* a teacher deal with a student they dislike? Well, the secret here is to try and avoid that dislike from happening in the first place. Occasionally it may be unavoidable, as the student may be dealing with issues far beyond the teacher's control and will exhibit disruptive behaviors despite the best efforts of the teacher to curtail them. Those rare cases will be addressed later in the chapter. But for your everyday, average attention-seeker, there are strategies that can be employed early in the student-teacher relationship to help stave off future tension. Of course, some strategies should be avoided, as we have learned the hard way.

COMMON MISTAKES MADE BY NEW TEACHERS IN REGARD TO DISCIPLINE

Discipline is probably the greatest source of anxiety for new teachers. Students can smell that anxiety oozing from your pores, and they will absolutely attempt to test your limits. As a result, you are bound to make mistakes on the road to becoming a disciplinarian. Here are some examples of some of the most common:

Having Classroom Rules That Are Too Strict and Therefore Seemingly Unreasonable When a Situation Arises. Assigning detention to every kid that is not in his or her seat at the late bell sounds great on paper, but thanks to increasing enrollment in today's already overcrowded school buildings, it may not be physically possible for certain kids to make it from one end of the building to the other in four minutes. Implementing rigid rules like this will paint you into a corner. That is not to say that kids should not be held accountable for tardiness, but the punishment should fit the crime. Don't worry; the kids will be rushing to your class on the first few days of school as they continue to "feel you out." You will get a pretty good idea of which students are trying to take advantage and which ones have a legitimate problem.

Not Having Clearly Stated Expectations and Consequences. No matter how bad your professional sports team of choice may look on any given Sunday, they never make things up as they go along. An immense amount of preparation goes into each and every play they make. The same goes for teaching. What works in the backyard after Thanksgiving dinner will not necessarily translate into the classroom. Students should know right from the beginning what the consequences of their actions will be. Calling the parent of one child who cheats on a test and assigning an essay to another does not only demonstrate your lack of organization to the students, it is also unfair, and the students will let you know about it.

Failing to Adhere to Disciplinary Action When Incidents Arise. This one can be avoided by having *reasonable*, not rigid, classroom rules. There will be times when you will not want to deal with a problem. This could be for any number of reasons. Perhaps you are simply tired, or you have a backlog of student work, or, more important, tickets to the "big game." Unfortunately, students don't factor those things in when they misbehave, and you cannot afford to "look the other way" because you will pay for it later, perhaps in the form of a reputation for being a "pushover."

Raising Your Voice at Students in Situations Other Than Times When Student Safety Is Severely Compromised. We absolutely guarantee that yelling at students (as much as they might deserve it) will *not* result in their being intimidated into submission. In fact, the opposite effect will occur. Instead of being scared of you, they will make fun of you. Teenagers love getting a rise out of new teachers. It makes them feel as if they have conquered uncharted territory. When they discover the X that marks the spot to your temper button, they will search for it time and again. It will be funnier to them each time you blow your top, and it will result in a very long year.

Allowing Students to See Which Kids Are Your "Favorites." We all have our "go-to" kids who we know will have something to say when the rest of the class is busy drooling and making paper airplanes. As much as they deserve to be recognized for their greatness, the rest of the class can misinterpret the lack of attention they receive as dislike for them. Remember, there are kids who would love to contribute to the class but may be too shy or nervous. Without realizing it, you could be hurting some of the other kids by showering a select few with attention.

Giving Students "Opportunity." Students will notice how much you pay attention, and they will get away with whatever they think they can (even that favorite student of yours). This behavior can be as innocuous as note passing and severe as a full class cheating on a test. You will end up looking as foolish as you allow yourself to look. Think about it . . . if the whole class cheats, what action do you take? You certainly don't want to bring that one to your boss, and the kids know that. They will not take your punishment seriously, and you are stuck in an impossible situation.

Forgetting Your Sense of Humor. Sometimes kids say things that poke a little fun at what you considered a serious discussion. If it is harmless, laugh! But remember, class clowns are always looking for a stage to work on their "A" material. Don't allow your classroom to turn into one. Make it clear that an occasional joke is okay, but you are still the boss. Don't turn the reins over to your budding comedian.

Overestimating Your Sense of Humor. Discipline strategies, like the use of sarcastic humor, that work for veteran teachers may not be appropriate for rookies. Every school has its "old-guard" types who get away with even the most politically incorrect behavior.

One of our more experienced colleagues has a unique way of communicating his displeasure with his students. When student work is bad, he will hold it up and tell them, "I wouldn't wipe my ass with these papers!" Kids think he is hilarious, and they often mildly act out just to see what he'll say next. The administration leaves him alone because he speaks to them the same way. Yes, he is popular with both kids and teachers. Yes, this strategy works for him. However, we have yet to see a new teacher who could (or should) pull off the same behavior. He's been at it a long time and knows what works for him. You don't, and it will take a few years before you do.

Sharing Too Much/Not Enough Personal Information. Newer, younger teachers are fascinating creatures to high school and middle school kids. They will want to know all about you, and what you don't tell them they will make up. I was twenty-two when I started teaching high school. After the first few days the questions started coming, the two most popular being, "Where do you live?" and "Do you have a boyfriend?" During the first couple of periods I glared at the class (remember, I wasn't planning on smiling until December) and said, "None of your business. Now, going back to *Of Mice and Men* . . ."

Their curiosity was only heightened by my response. When I decided to answer honestly during another period, my answers of, "Yes, his name is Tom and we met in college" and "in the Riverdale section of the Bronx" allowed them to move on much more easily. All the same, a much worse offense is trying to tell them *everything* about yourself. Students want to know a little about your wedding, pets, sister, roommates, travels, and so forth. However, at some point they are only asking you these questions to get out of moving on with the class. And those of you who think it is appropriate to complain to students about hangovers and brag about your social life deserve the discipline problems that follow.

The examples listed above are the more common mistakes the new teacher will make. Unfortunately, much more serious, even potentially dangerous, examples arise from time to time. The most extreme cases are discussed in chapter 7 on violence. The following incidents, while not necessarily life-threatening, had the potential to escalate and were completely our responsibility. Fortunately for you, we have already committed these blunders that could have easily been avoided had we been armed with more experience. As you read the case studies, think about what could have been done differently. Suggestions from one of our resident administrators will follow.

CASE STUDIES

Case One: Chris Gets Burned for "Just Doing His Job"

People like to be noticed. They wear trendy clothes, they get their hair done a certain way, they excel in sports, they try their hand at acting, and they even write books. Kids are no exception. As they find themselves spending a good portion of their youth in school, it's obvious they will be looking to stand out in that environment. Most of the time, they do it in relatively benign fashion, through things like the aforementioned trendy clothes and hairstyles. Of course, even these can lead to awkward moments.

I recall one particularly hot, steamy afternoon in June during my second full year of teaching. The faculty had been urged by our principal to enforce the school's dress code. Essentially, it meant to tell the girls to put their clothes back on. If they forgot to bring clothes that day, they were to be sent to the office and they would be given a T-shirt. In case I'm being less than literal, let me qualify my previous statements. In the summertime, people are apt to wear less, males and females included. However, in my modest experience, or perhaps just from having a male perspective, I found that the females that graced our halls during such weather had a tendency to reveal quite a bit of themselves. And by "themselves" I mean shoulders, cleavage, and the occasional plumber's crack (I believe it is now referred to as a "coin slot").

Now, being a young, eager teacher and wanting to impress my principal, I quickly found my opportunity to play clothing cop. I noticed a young woman walking with her friends in the hallway who looked like she just stepped out of a burlesque show. I approached her, politely of course, and did my duty. As I recall, the conversation went something like this:

"Excuse me, young lady?"

"What?"

"Would you mind putting something on?"

"What?"

"You're violating the dress code. You need to cover yourself up."

Up until now, everything was going fine. By the book, you might say. I approached her in a nonconfrontational way and very calmly asked her to comply with the dress code. Had I known she was about to channel Ethel Merman, I might have approached the situation differently: "Ewww! Why you *loo*-kin'? This crazy-ass teacher is looking at my boobs! Y'all better get out my face before I sue you!"

That was clearly not the response I had expected. As you may have guessed, I suddenly found myself quite speechless. The young lady and her entourage continued on their merry way, enjoying a laugh at my expense.

Case Two: Remember . . . You Kiss Your Mother with That Mouth

During my first full year working in the South Bronx, I tried to speak to an unruly young man "on his level" by employing a bit of colloquial speech that is never to be uttered from a teacher's mouth. On this particular day, this young man was literally running around the room, throwing things, pushing other kids, and generally ignoring my every word. When I finally got his attention, I pulled him aside and, stupidly, asked him to stop "f'ing around." It was now his turn to channel Nathan Lane: "Oh! Teacher says he wants to f#^* me!"

If you learn anything from this book, please make sure it is never to say f#^*.

Case Three: Amy's Movie Marathon

I swear I wasn't being lazy. I really wanted the kids to know this stuff. We began a unit on Ernest Hemingway, and I thought that instead of my lecturing on the author's truly fascinating life, I would show my tenth graders one of my favorite Hemingway documentaries. It was a cable special; its running time was about 120 minutes. That would fit nicely into three 42-minute classes! The students asked if they needed to take notes, and because I was not going to quiz them I told them to just watch. My popularity soared!

The students were great the first day. By the second day, they were great during the more exciting scenes that focused on Hemingway's try at bullfighting and his reputation as a ladies' man. However, on day three, things got ugly. In one particular class, the students had fits of hysterical laughter when the documentary brought up the fact that Gertrude Stein, Hemingway's mentor, was a lesbian. One boy in the back kept chanting, "Ger-trude-Stein . . . Les-bi-an! Ger-trude-Stein! Les-bi-an!"

I responded, "Michael, that's enough. Please watch the movie." Short-lived silence.

Michael: "Ger-trude-Stein . . . Les-bi-an! Ger-trude-Stein! Les-bi-an!"

Me: "Michael, I said that is enough."

Finally the movie ended with a bit of time left in the period. I asked the class what they thought was the most fascinating aspect of Hemingway's life. I'm sure you can guess the answer that flew out of one of Michael's buddy's mouths.

I told them that Stein's sexual orientation was not up for discussion, as it would have little bearing on the upcoming unit on *The Old Man and the Sea*. No one was listening to me, and although they weren't, it seemed as if the entire class was now chanting, "Ger-trude-Stein . . . Les-bi-an! Ger-trude-Stein! Les-bi-an!" I finally hollered, "Enough about lesbians!" and went to kick Michael and his friend out of class. Of course, the bell rang and the kids skipped victoriously out of the room, knowing they had evaded punishment and excited from getting a rise out of me. To make matters even worse, I went to my mailbox later that day to find a note that said, "Dear Ms. Sutton: It is clear to me that you are homophobic. Your obvious dislike for lesbians is childish, ultraconservative, and racist. Anonymous."

ADMINISTRATIVE ANALYSIS

Case One

Chris did several things wrong. First and foremost, he challenged this young woman in front of her friends. No one wants to lose face, particularly when surrounded by his or her peers. Had he asked her to step away from the group for a moment and kept it confidential, she may have been more receptive. Also, he spoke to her like a robot. "Danger! Danger! Dress code violation, Will Robinson!" People don't respond well when spoken down to, adolescents in particular. A more informal, conversational tone and a bit of humor could have made all the difference. Of course, informal and conversational can also be disastrous, as illustrated in Case Two.

Case Two

Obviously, Chris made a poor decision. When behavior is considered unacceptable for a student, teachers should remember they are held to an even higher standard that needs to be maintained at all costs. Clearly his intention was to speak in a way with which the student could identify. However, first and foremost the student should be able to identify his teacher as an adult.

As tempting as it is to try to make a point by speaking to them "on their level," great care must be taken to ensure that the situation does not get more out of control than it already is. If the situation was truly as bad as Chris said, safety was certainly an issue and he should not have tried to handle it alone. As much as new teachers are hesitant to ask for help for fear of it reflecting poorly on them, that is, after all, what administrators are there for. No teacher is expected to single-handedly deal with a student who is intent on disrupting the learning process, not to mention destroying school property.

Case Three

Amy's first mistake was poor use of classroom time. Kids love videos, and they are a great learning tool. However, no group of kids can sit through three class periods of a documentary without getting restless. After all, boredom is fertile ground for misbehavior.

Her second mistake was not holding students accountable. Why should they pay attention to the movie? What was in it for them? Asking them to take notes and assigning a quiz would have kept them on task for a longer period of time. Finally, the inappropriate references to lesbians should have been addressed. It must be made clear that intolerance toward any group of people is unacceptable in the classroom. Most schools have clear rules regarding this. As for the letter portraying Amy as insensitive, it is understandable that the anonymous student came to that conclusion when she did not take a solid stand against the offending students' behavior.

FINAL TIPS ON DISCIPLINE

You can avoid many discipline problems with engaging lesson plans. Nevertheless, consistently coming up with engaging lesson plans is *way* easier said than done. However, if students feel a slight pressure to pay attention (because they know there will be a quiz on the notes) and if activities are geared so that the class moves at a lively, interesting pace and a variety of activities like lectures, seat work, and discussions are included, kids will not become as bored and will not look to entertain themselves and each other as much.

Clear expectations and a predictable routine are essential for an ordered classroom. If students know what to expect from the class, the class routine will become habit. Of course, after a few months you should change things up (including the seating chart) to refresh everyone a little. In addition, if they know that cheating on a test will result in a zero, and one kid cheats and word gets around that he received that zero, fewer kids will be likely to test the waters.

Remember you are not their friend. If you act too much like a "buddy" to the kids, which is so tempting because it is fun to be "liked," you are setting yourself up for major failure. Even though they like you, they will test your limits; and when you "punish" them, they will feel betrayed and will no longer trust you. Those kids who adored you and made you feel like the coolest person who ever walked through the door will make your life as miserable as they can. They will avoid participating in class discussions, and they will roll their eyes (or worse) when you try to engage them.

Keep cool. If you have a hot temper and large (fragile) ego, remember you are dealing with children. There are few things as exciting to kids as pushing a teacher's buttons. If they get a rise out of you, it will be all the talk in the cafeteria and in other teachers' classrooms. You will develop a hot-under-the-collar reputation among both students and faculty, probably complete with an insulting nickname. If you are starting to lose control of a situation and would like to avoid involving an administrator, simply ask the student to leave the room. If you are concerned with the effect this may have on the student, rest assured he or she has probably been through this before, and his or her self-esteem will most likely remain intact.

Depending on your school's policies, you can:

- Have the student stand outside the doorway of your classroom. This way you can keep an eye on the offender until you find an opportunity to talk with him or her privately.
- Keep an "emergency" assignment in your desk and have an arrangement with a fellow teacher in which you can send your unruly student to sit with his or her class, preferably of another age group. No senior wants to deal with the embarrassment of being sent to a freshman classroom, and freshmen quite often feel intimidated by upperclassmen.

Obviously, there is no way to predict every unfortunate incident that a teacher will face. Hopefully, the information provided in this chapter will help the inexperienced teacher sense when one of those incidents is about to occur. Being prepared so that disciplinary problems are avoided in the first place will certainly make your life easier. In addition to that, an important phrase to remember is "praise in public, punish in private." If students are behaving well, let them know it. Say something like: "You all seem to be working very hard. Well done!" A little positive reinforcement goes a long way.

Finally, remember that you are not alone in this. Administrators get paid exorbitant amounts of money to do what they do. And, contrary to what some may think, most of them are there to help you. Of course, some situations may require the involvement of parents, and that is a joy that will be discussed in the next chapter.

5

HELLO, MOTHER; HELLO, FATHER (HELLO, NANNY; HELLO LEGAL GUARDIAN): DEALING WITH PARENTS

Michael Corleone said it best: Never go against the family. The same rules apply when dealing with the parents of your students. When dealt with properly, they can be your strongest allies. When not, they can make a surprise visit to your class by the superintendent on the one day you decide to "wing it" look like a box social. Don't forget, you're not handling their financial portfolio, you're teaching their kids. Assuming that the education of their children is high on their list of priorities (which, sadly, is not always the case), expect them to get involved if there is an issue at school.

Of course, not all parents will show this level of enthusiasm when their help is requested. A good determiner is the audible groan on the other end of the phone when they find out what the call is about. When you hear that, chances are they've been down this road before with at least one other teacher, and they've long since stopped leaving a trail of bread crumbs for you to follow.

Parental involvement is one of those facets of teaching that remains a constant challenge to even the most experienced educators. It's like the proverbial box of chocolates: You never know what you are going to get when you pick up the phone for the first time. Will he or she be the supportive, conscientious type whose jaw will drop at the very idea of his or her child doing something wrong at school? Or will you get what we call the "student's best friend," the parent that seems to think his or her child is the kid brother or sister he or she never had and must be defended at all costs, regardless of the devastation they may be causing at school? Of course, you could find yourself tangling with a shape-shifter, the kind that thanks you and agrees with you on the phone and then blames everything on you when they come in for a meeting with an administrator.

These factors are enough to keep teachers from asking parents for help, and that's unfortunate, because parents should know what their kids are up to. Of course, some parental interaction can be unavoidable. There are parents that seem to make a hobby out of tracking their child's teacher down so they can relay the child's strengths, weaknesses, hopes, dreams, allergies, phobias, taste in music, shoe size, or whatever else they have determined you must know in order to properly educate their child. And of course, there is report card time, when your phone will ring and your e-mail box will be filled to bursting because parents want to know why their child isn't performing well and just what the hell you are going to do about it. Make sure your grade book is up to snuff when this happens, unless you want to end up sleeping with the fishes.

PARENTS 101: KNOW WHAT YOU ARE GETTING INTO

The majority of parents will look to work *with* you when you call them regarding their child's behavior or academics. You will need no help with that population. In fact, after hanging up with a cooperative parent, you will feel validated and inspired to do everything you can to make that parent happy, which you can do by doing everything you can to work with their child to solve the problem at hand. Unfortunately, there will be those *other* parents, and they fall into two categories: the obnoxiously unreasonable and the pathetically underinvolved.

The obnoxiously unreasonable are dangerous—they can single-handedly ruin an otherwise successful year. The underinvolved will break your heart, and their lack of interest in their child explains the student's undesirable behavior. That being said, you and your school's team of experts (guidance counselors, coaches, psychologists) are on your own to solve the problem you are having with the student.

COMMON MISTAKES MADE BY THE NEW TEACHER IN REGARD TO UNREASONABLE PARENTS

Trying to Deal with an Unreasonable Parent on Your Own. Your first lines of defense are those trusty veteran teachers. Chances are, if the parent is *that* bad, some other poor soul will have had an unfortunate experience with them at some point. They may be able to tell you what worked for them and, more importantly, what did *not* work for them.

Assuming That Anything You Do, Short of Doing Things Exactly the Way They Want You to, Will Appease Them. The most unreasonable of parents will not be satisfied by a compromise. They want things done their way, and if they have to go to the superintendent to get it, they will. The unreasonable parent is a shameless creature that craves victory. At first they want "what's best for their child." However, it often turns into a competition they are intent upon "winning."

Meeting with Them without a Guidance Counselor or Administrator Present. This is one of the greatest mistakes in the history of new teachers. New teachers, rightly or wrongly, have it in their heads that getting the administration involved in an incident reflects poorly on their professional abilities. While this is true if you call the principal every time a note is passed or homework is missed, it is not when the stakes are high. Having a "witness," as dramatic as that sounds, is important. Think about it; a parent cannot call a principal or counselor and exaggerate things that may have been said if there is someone there to give a true account of the meeting. In addition, the third-party can also work as the meeting facilitator, keeping the tone appropriate and the pace reasonable.

Trashing the Parent to Other Parents, Kids, or Even a Faculty Member You Don't Know Well. Temptation, thy name is gossip. When a parent and teacher are involved in a heated incident, word travels fast among the faculty and the community. We have seen it happen, especially to coaches. Other parents who may have their own agenda or who may truly think they are offering support often pull the victimized teacher aside and say something like: "I heard about what is going on with Crazy Mrs. X. What a shame. You know we are on your side. How are things going with that, anyway?" While the temptation to jump into the other parent's arms and tell her just how terrible your life has been since the drama with Mrs. X began is enormous, you must fight the urge and reply, "Thank you, we're working it out."

Taking Out Your Anger with the Parent on the Child. As teachers, it is a necessity of our profession that we forgive students time and time again. When an incident occurs, you have to adopt the theory that tomorrow is another day and move on. Of course, this is much easier said than done when the parents have not moved on and they are making your life miserable. It is hard not to try to deflect that misery in the student's direction, but it would simply be inappropriate. You cannot, for example, bring in Halloween candy for the entire class and when little Brenda asks why she can't have any say, "Because your mother sucks, that's why." The same goes for grades. You have to be as objective as ever. You cannot fail a student, ignore her, or make her sit by the garbage can or partner her up with the smelly kid just because her parents are evil.

Not Keeping Accurate and Thorough Records. When dealing with insane parents, you must have every phone call and e-mail documented. These people are just nuts enough to make things up, like saying you did not return their phone calls when you actually did. In addition, you may want to photocopy the student's assignments before handing them back. Do not put it past wacky parents to try to change a paper's content after it is handed back to show how unfairly you treated their son or daughter.

After you finish grading it, photocopy it and put it in a safe place. Hand the original back to the student, and if the mom or dad tries to mess with you by adding a paragraph that makes the paper a slam dunk, you can sit back and enjoy the show of the color draining from their faces as you prove their lunacy once and for all by producing the photocopied original. We have seen this happen, and there is no sweeter victory, and your administrator will be highly impressed (and possibly a bit frightened) at your cunning.

Allowing a Phone Conversation to Go in Circles. Nutty parents will not shut up until they get their way, and their way is most likely highly unreasonable and impossible to comply with. Your time is too precious to waste going over the same points one hundred times in a row. In addition, if it is a crowded free period in the teachers' lounge, there is no doubt a line of teachers waiting to call parents, spouses, bookies, and therapists, and they don't need to wait for the new guy to finish getting trampled by some kid's dad to make their phone calls.

Losing Your Temper. If you lose your temper, the parents have officially won, and since crazed parents are all about holding out for victory, you don't want that. It will make it almost impossible for your administrator or union rep to come to your defense if you start yelling and, even worse, cursing, so just don't do it.

There is also something very powerful about not letting someone who is trying to provoke you accomplish that. The parent is often dying for you to lose your cool, and the longer you stay calm while they are ranting and raving the more irate they will get. They will look worse while you look better.

Allowing the Student to Breeze through Your Class Because You Have Lost the Endurance to Fight with the Parent. This is an easy trap to fall into. Although it is not fair, you must know that if you are unfortunate enough to have the offspring of an evil parent in your class, the battle may last throughout the entire year. It is often their goal to wear you down to the point of compliance, and while that is the easy way out, it is unfair to the other students in your class.

We will be honest: Other teachers will encourage you to "just give in" so that you have a peaceful year, and you will notice that some of the student's other teachers will do just that. That makes your job even more difficult, because the parents will constantly come at you and your supervisors with points like "Well, she just doesn't seem to be having these problems in Mr. Smith's class." Rest assured, if Mr. Smith and teachers like him were doing their job, those problems would come to light. Just grade and treat the student the way he or she deserves to be graded or treated, and deal with the consequences.

COMMON MISTAKES MADE BY THE NEW TEACHER IN REGARD TO THE UNDERINVOLVED PARENT

Giving Up on the Child. When nobody at home cares about a student, it is so easy to let him or her slip through the cracks because no one is going to bother you about the situation. If you teach in high school or middle school, you probably have between 100 and 150 students to worry about, and letting a few go may seem inevitable. However, that is just not an option. You have to praise, grade, reprimand, and get to know each of your students appropriately, and that goes double for those who seem to be on their own. They may or may not care about how they do in your class, but they need to know that you do.

Thinking You Can Inspire the Parent to Care. You can tell the parents all night long how wonderful their child's science lab or essay was, but most likely they won't care. If they do, and it is because of what you said, you can pat yourself on the back for an outstanding accomplishment. However, if the parent requests that you leave him or her alone and refrain from calling, you must comply.

CASE STUDIES

Case One: Cheaters

As teachers, we are not only educators, we are also the morality police. When we see injustice brewing in our classrooms, it is our job to quell it before it spreads to the innocent children surrounding the culprits. In the spirit of it "taking a village" to raise a child, we believe that parents should be thrilled to know that their children's teachers are there to foster academic and moral well-being from 7:30 a.m. to 2:30 p.m. every day. Well, not all parents believe this is in a teacher's job description and would rather banish the teacher from the village than have him or her teaching their children to accept responsibility when they are wrong. What makes it worse is when that parent is one of the scariest of the village leaders, a school board member.

During my first year I assigned an essay to one of my classes that I regarded as a minor assignment. Most students completed it easily, and we went on with our lives. However, one student, whom we will call Jerry, was absent when the assignment was given, and by the time he made it up, I had graded the rest of the class's essays and was ready to return them. For some reason, most probably my extreme lack of organization, I kept forgetting to hand them back to the class. When I read Jerry's, it immediately sounded familiar, so I dug through the pile, where I found a perfect match. It was already graded (it received a 95) and was written by a student named Fred. When I was discussing the situation in the teachers' lounge, I was horrified to hear one of the elder statesmen say, "Aren't they both board members' sons? Good luck with that one, little girl."

I immediately told my assistant principal, and we decided to give "the copier" a zero and take twenty-five points off "the supplier's" grade. After calculating how these punishments would affect their overall quarter grades, we discovered that Fred would still get a high "B" or even an "A" and that Jerry would still easily pass. I decided to call the parents.

Jerry's parents could not have been more apologetic, embarrassed, and accepting of the penalty. They even made the kid stay after with me and write it over. The student, who never acted out before, remained his polite, pleasant self for the rest of the year and was truly ashamed of his actions. Unfortunately, things did not go as well with Fred's absolutely psychotic mother, and it became clear as the year went on that the apple did not fall far from the insanity tree.

When I called Fred's mom, I was completely taken back when she *immediately* went on about how unfair it was that Fred should lose points on his paper. Little did she know the administrator wanted to give him a zero, stating that cheating was cheating whether or not you copied someone else's work or supplied your work to be copied. Not only did she go off on the stupidity of the policy, she also went off on me personally, saying that she had been so excited that Fred had a young new teacher and that she had had high hopes that I would have innovative lessons and ways of thinking.

She continued by saying that she had a feeling she was wrong when Fred would come home complaining about how boring English was, but now she was convinced of it, seeing how I was on a power trip and was taking it out on an innocent boy. In addition, she added, did I think it was appropriate to punish a student when all he was trying to do was *help* a weaker boy?

All of this was said before she even took her first breath. I tried to defend myself, first by telling her that I was sorry that Fred thought English was boring and that maybe he would enjoy it more when we moved on to a different novel or perhaps a play. I went on and on about all the fabulous ideas for making the literature more interesting and getting the kids excited about writing. I also mentioned that Jerry was not a weak student; he simply made a poor decision when he chose to copy Fred's paper.

This set her off even more, with her going on about how none of that was the point and she did not understand why I brought it up. She ended the phone call with an inspiring, uplifting point about the fact that if the boys hadn't viewed me as stupid in the first place, they never would have tried to pull off something like this. I was about to explain to her that I was obviously not stupid because I had caught them when she conveniently informed me that she had to go.

I was completely freaked out over the affair, but I thought that the worst was, at least, over. I guess the boys were right; I was stupid because that was really just the beginning.

After exposing Fred for the cheater that he was, his mother proceeded to call me every day for approximately one month. I remember it was February, so at least it was a short month. I took each and every one of her calls, during which she would find some new way to insult me. Some days she would say that I was only taking twenty-five points off the paper because Fred was a boy, and everyone knew I favored the girls. Sometimes she would say it was because Fred was a basketball player, and she had heard through the grapevine that I did not like athletes.

During each phone call I would defend myself while my colleagues sat back microwaving their Lean Cuisines and munching their turkey sandwiches, and I grew more and more pathetic. Of course, I would always suggest that if she really had a problem she should try contacting the assistant principal, but she explained she had tried and that he was not budging on the twenty-five points because he had a thing for new young teachers. She really was a live one.

March came, and the phone calls stopped, but the e-mails started. She would e-mail quotes from her calendar about inspiring teachers and then add, "However, that is not you" to the bottom. While these e-mails stressed me out beyond belief, my buddies in the English department found them quite amusing. At the start of our daily lunch period, they would not eat their frozen dinners until I checked my e-mail so they could see what "that crazy witch had to say now." I would laugh nervously along with them, but I knew this was spiraling out of control. What made me feel worse was the fact that I had not really involved an administrator since the first week in February.

The e-mails continued. Fred would turn in all of his work in class, but he would never speak or raise his hand. I had almost begun to share my colleagues' amusement when the situation got worse than I could have possibly imagined.

My assistant principal wanted to meet with me, and when I stopped by my mailbox on the way, I immediately knew why. In it was a twelve-page letter to the superintendent, copied to the building principal, Fred's guidance counselor, the assistant principal, and me. In it was documentation of phone calls, containing "records" of things I never said. In addition, there was a list of supposed offenses I committed against her son, including going to his basketball games to heckle him and specifically cheer loudly for his fellow players in order to make him feel bad.

The assistant principal was not mad at me, because there was no denying that this lady was completely insane. Nevertheless, he was disappointed that I let it get to this level without my informing him of the situation. The superintendent had called him and asked him what was going on, inquiring whether this lady was really as nuts as she seemed or if this Ms. Sutton was as incompetent as she was saying. Obviously, the assistant principal stood up for me and the superintendent assumed correctly that it was another case of a crazy mother. He knew the father from the school board and said he was not surprised.

I guess the superintendent never responded to her letter and eventually there were no more e-mails about how uninspiring I was. I was thrilled when the last day of school came, but I was silly to assume that the situation was behind me. Fred's guidance counselor stopped me on my way out, and she showed me a petition asking the principal to fire me that Fred had passed around the school. She said she thought it was something I should see, but afterward tore it up and threw it out, explaining that it was garbage. I was happy to see that only two other students had signed (I had 140 that year), but it was a rough reminder of how easily things can get out of control.

Case Two: The Truth Hurts (So Much)

While it has been my pleasure to teach many gifted writers over the years, it must be pointed out that every once in a while a child will come along whose powers in that area far exceed those of the rest. This is the kid that you know will be a professional writer someday. I once had an encounter with a young man with writing ability of this caliber. Unfortunately, I allowed my own insecurities as a teacher and as a person to get in the way of properly recognizing that talent and as a result permanently damaged my relationship with that student and his parent.

He was a wiseass; of that there can be no doubt. While most of his daily ribbing of me was good natured, there were occasions where I felt the boy was treading dangerously close to the "line" we say should not be crossed, perhaps with a comment about my physical appearance, for example. Now, being a plus-sized guy, I was used to this sort of humor and I would respond to such remarks with carefully worded comebacks of my own, sometimes coming a little too close to that "line" myself. And this is how our daily meetings would go, at least until the young man decided to entertain himself by writing an essay on a subject I could not tolerate so easily: my teaching ability.

What I found ironic about this is that the young man was incredibly anxious for me to read his paper. Being in no particular hurry to accommodate a person that was a considerable cause of grief to me, I may have inadvertently allowed his essay to wind up at the bottom of my stack. He would ask me about it daily: "Mr. Purr, have you read my essay yet?"

I would respond the exact way every day in a tone I thought he deserved: "Not yet. I'm sorry. Have you seen the size of this stack?"

Finally, I reached the bottom, and there it was. Knowing I probably wouldn't need it, I uncapped my red pen and sat down to see what all of the fuss was about. As I read, my eyes bulged out of my head and my breathing became short. I had barely finished the last line when I found myself running down to see the boy's house principal, the essay clutched in my hand like the "smoking gun" I needed to finally see that justice was bestowed upon this little fiend. I handed it to the administrator and watched gleefully as he read it, my eyes following his as he went from line to line. When he finished, he did not smirk as I did, but instead looked somewhat perplexed: "Okay, so you're telling me that you're offended by this, right?"

Was he kidding? It was all there in black and white! "Absolutely! He has gone out of his way to not only insult my teaching ability, but he makes thinly veiled remarks about minorities as well! He should be suspended!"

The administrator looked at the essay for a moment and then gave a slight nod, as if he were doing something against his better judgment: "Here's what I'll do. I'll assign him one day of in-school suspension, but I need you to do something for me. Call his parents and let them know about it. They should probably hear from you directly on this one."

Even though I felt like he was passing the buck to me about the phone call, I agreed, no doubt because of the anger that was swelling within me. And what could a child say in an essay that could enrage a teacher so? Essentially, he described my classroom like a town in the Old West, completely out of control. He also used my own anecdotes against me as he incorporated references to the "wild animal" children I had taught in the Bronx. While I don't recall ever referring to them as "wild animals," when my suburban, sheltered students would ask about my days working in the "ghetto" as they called it, I was guilty of telling them stories of those days, a practice I have since ceased.

To add insult to injury, he portrayed himself as the dashing hero of the piece, and I was the aging, ineffective sheriff he was there to replace. I stamped out his number on the phone keypad and took a deep breath as I waited to vent on the parent for the actions of the child. The conversation, with the boy's father, went something like this:

"What can I do for you, Mr. Purr?"

"I'm sorry to tell you that your son is going to be suspended for something he did in English class."

"Really? He's never been suspended before. What did he do?"

"Well, it's not so much what he did as what he wrote."

"He's being suspended for something he wrote?"

"Yes sir. I just wanted to let you know so that . . . "

"What did he write?"

Suddenly, putting the horrible event into words got very difficult: "Well, basically, he wrote an essay where he, well, made fun of me."

"Oh, yes, I read that essay. I thought it was pretty good. He mentioned it was taking you an unusually long time to get it back to him."

We've all had that anxiety-laden dream where we're riding a city bus naked. As I sat there on the phone, I suddenly felt the urge to cover up my vitals: "Yes, well, I have a large number of writing students this term and it's been difficult to . . . "

"So what was wrong with the essay, Mr. Purr?"

In a matter of seconds I had gone from predator to prey: "Well, it was very disrespectful."

"Really? How so?"

"He implied my classroom was out of control."

"Well, I'm sure it's not, is it?"

This guy was good. The apple didn't fall far from the tree in that family. I was clearly in over my head. In my mind I had visions of the other jokers in that class that drove me nuts on a daily basis. Maybe it was out of control. I suddenly had the urge to say, "Sorry, wrong number!" and hang up the phone. Of course, escape was impossible: "No, no, of course not. That's not the point. The point is . . . "

"My son is rather fond of your class, Mr. Purr. He says the atmosphere is, how did he say it, light-hearted, but in a positive way."

Okay, so the guy knew I had no classroom control. Fine. I still had my race card to play: "I'm afraid there was more to it than that, sir. You see, he also refers to minorities in a negative way."

"Really? I don't recall reading anything like that."

I felt the momentum returning to my side. I fired my final salvo: "He refers to them as 'wild animals.'"

"You know, Mr. Purr, I asked him about those references. According to him, he was just referencing something he heard you say in class. In fact, I believe he had quote marks around those references. Is that something you said in class, Mr. Purr?"

In my own defense, I must point out that despite the fact that I witnessed extraordinary acts of misbehavior while I worked there, I cared very deeply for the kids I taught in the city. However, that being said, in the heat of the moment while telling one of my "war stories" in my new school, I may have in fact used words like that, to my shame.

"Mr. Purr, are you there?"

"Yes, sir, I'm here."

"Mr. Purr, are you sure it's my son that has the problem?"

"I think I'll have another look at the essay, sir, and I'll get back to you."

"That's sounds like a good idea, Mr. Purr. I look forward to hearing from you again."

Needless to say, there was no detention assigned.

Case Three: Oedipus Reborn

The saddest thing you can encounter as a teacher is a student who is seemingly not loved by his parents. The most nauseating thing is a student who is loved too much. My fourth year found me with a great deal to be excited about: I was tenured, I had been married over the summer, and I was partnered up for four of my classes with a special-education teacher, Jess, who happened to be one of my best friends. Everything was coming up Amy!

I have to admit our classes had some tough kids with unfortunate backgrounds, but Jess is a really talented person who has a special touch with those students. We had spent a great deal of time over the summer researching and attending workshops in order to prepare for the year ahead. However, nothing prepared us for Eddie and his mom. In fact, they left such an impression on us, we prefer to call him Oeddie.

Eddie fooled us in the beginning. While his skills in language arts were definitely weak, his attitude, intelligence, and support from his parents made him a model student in spite of his struggles with the subject. Eventually, though, things got ugly.

Eddie, it seemed, had a bit of an anger-management problem that did not show itself until later in the year. It turned out he had a crush on one of the young ladies in our class, but unfortunately the feelings were unrequited. He started to really harass this girl before and during class, and she actually came to us to intervene. Believing that this could be remedied with one call to his supportive mom, we were not worried.

The call did not go as expected. Mrs. Eddie was defensive of her son, and she immediately started blaming the girl, saying that she must be leading him on and that a boy his age with his hormones can't be expected to have control over himself when *she* is probably walking around half-naked and saying things to tease him. When we explained that the girl was doing nothing of the sort, she told us that she expected us to take the girl's side, being that we are, in fact, girls, and that we have no understanding of boys.

After that phone call, Eddie really started to act up in class. He would make obnoxious comments and refuse to do his work. Jess and I thought he may have been embarrassed, and that it was a phase. We let his house principal, who was in communication with his mom, know. However, one day Eddie and the object of his affection were having a little discussion during homeroom. Jess and I kept a close eye on them, when, all of a sudden, Eddie unzipped and dropped his pants. We told him to stop, settled the class down, and began to write him up when he actually did it again! His house principal decided his mother should come in for a meeting, and surely she couldn't take his side this time . . . right?

Wrong. The meeting was horrible. The principal was a bit tough on Eddie, because he had totally traumatized the girl when he dropped his pants *and* he was insubordinate when he dropped them for the second time. Both were unacceptable offenses. When the principal asked Jess and I to give our side of the story, Mrs. Eddie actually put her hand out to stop us. We thought she had finally come to her senses and was going to go on about how embarrassed she was. Instead, after we quieted down at her signal, she turned to her son, took his face in her hands, and said: "Edward, you and I are not going to listen to this. I love you. I *love* you and we can get through this, just you and me. That's what matters, and what matters is that I love you."

Eddie replied, "I love you, too, Mom. I knew you would never believe them."

Mrs. Eddie went on to say, "You were saying, ladies?"

Jess, the principal, and I sat stunned at the not-so-touching moment we had just witnessed. While we tried to go on with the meeting, it was obvious that nothing was going to make Mrs. Eddie hear what we had to say. In the end, we switched Eddie into a different class of ours so that the young lady he was harassing would no longer feel uncomfortable. He served out his punishment (a suspension) with great protest that included a letter of dissatisfaction from his mother sent to the superintendent regarding the way her son was treated. While he did his work reluctantly for the remainder of the year, he was not exactly what you would call "a pleasure to have in class."

ADMINISTRATIVE ANALYSIS

Case One

Amy's situation was a mess, and it is a realistic story but it should not be discouraging. While almost everybody encounters a parent this intense, it is usually only once (or twice) in a career. Hopefully, this was it for Amy. The administration should always be informed when a parent is harassing you, and this was absolutely harassment. The thing here was that Amy really did not do anything wrong, so she should have been more comfortable and confident about bringing this to a higher authority. There are a number of solutions that could have been employed here, starting with something as simple as a phone call from the principal to the parent to something as severe as moving the student to another teacher's class.

Amy's response to the overaggressive parent, while understandable, was inappropriate. As a person worried about keeping her job and getting tenure, she was unable to see how this incident was monopolizing not only her time but also the phone, which needed to be shared by other faculty members. Amy could have better spent the time dealing with this mother by working with other students, grading papers, or creating lessons. Valuable time was wasted because she was not prepared to deal with a domineering parent.

As for Amy's concern about her reputation, it was certainly well founded, but unnecessary. While administrators take each parental and student concern seriously, we understand that some people are just plain unreasonable, and unless a number of parents have the same complaint, we usually ignore the ranting after a while, and we certainly don't hold it against our teachers.

Case Two

What makes this case so complex is the fact that the essay refers to the classroom teacher in what Chris describes as an insulting way. There will be times in a teacher's career when this sort of unacceptable behavior will indeed occur, and it should be dealt with accordingly. However, this is not one of those cases. While it may have seemed that the essay the boy wrote (which I have read and can tell you is quite good) was about Chris, it really wasn't. It was about a boy looking to show off his writing ability to a teacher he thought would appreciate it. What Chris did wrong was something far too many educators do: They take something like this personally. As a result, he let his anger cloud his judgment. The house principal was absolutely right to have Chris call the child's parent, a task he failed miserably. In fact, it was a perfect example of what not to do when calling Mom or Dad. He rushed to make the call while he was still angry and did not take any time to collect his thoughts. As a result, he found himself at a disadvantage during the entire conversation. You might be in a situation where you have every justification in the world for calling a parent about a student's behavior, but if you call when you're angry, you will probably not get your facts straight and will sound quite unprofessional. It can also cause the parent to become angry and then you have a real disaster on your hands. Fortunately for Chris, the parent he called knew what his child had written and was somewhat prepared for the phone call. Many times, however, parents may not be as informed ahead of time, so be careful with how you present yourself.

Another thing to point out is the fact that the parent in this case clearly had the upper hand in this conversation and Chris ended up looking rather foolish. While Chris may have deserved just that in this particular case, that is not something you want to have happen to you on a regular basis. Not all parents are as receptive as the one Chris encountered. Know what you are going to say before you say it. Write down important points that you can refer to when making contact. Be prepared to listen to parents' questions and concerns. A parent has every right to be concerned when his or her child is in trouble. Just remember to be properly prepared before you speak to them.

Case Three

Amy's case, while highly stressful for her, was not something to get upset over. In fact, any administrator with even a small sense of humor would be able to laugh at the events of that meeting along with the two teachers.

What is not funny is the harassment of the young lady in the class, and the priority was ensuring that she could be made to feel comfortable. Switching the classes and punishing Eddie were the only two realistic solutions. While I am sure that Amy and Jess would have preferred to have Eddie removed from their roster, moving a kid around midyear complicates things for teachers and students alike, and since Mrs. Eddie did not push for a change, it was appropriate that he remain with them.

FINAL TIPS FOR DEALING WITH PARENTS

Try to have a "witness" in the room whenever you speak with the parent, preferably your department chair or a guidance counselor. As stated before, keep pristine records. Teach your class as if it is being recorded, because thanks to modern technology, it just might be. Actually, having this mind-set will keep your lessons sharp and meaningful.

When a phone call gets out of hand, and it may, simply say to the parent, "Mr. X, I apologize but I must cut this short. I must meet with a student. Perhaps you can e-mail your concerns?" This will provide you with a record of the unreasonable complaints and it will give you time to formulate an appropriate, well-thought-out response with the help of your colleagues or an administrator.

Know when to surrender. Many would disagree with this advice, but it is a realistic suggestion. Keep the goal in mind. If the child has not handed in a bunch of assignments and the parent wants him or her to be able to make them up instead of taking zeros, you may have to let the student do so. In the end, the goal was for the kid to learn the stuff, right? Hold him or her accountable for *every* missed assignment and provide a reasonable due date. Make up a contract signed by the parent, the principal, the student, and yourself. The student may want extra help, and offer no more or no less than your contract dictates. If the student meets the requirements, the parent has absolutely no right to complain anymore and the principal will certainly not require you to do any more favors for the family. If the student does not comply, then the parent does not have a leg to stand on and it goes on record that you did everything in your power to help him or her pass.

Do not let the idea of encountering a vitriolic parent discourage you. Everyone has their share of run-ins with this animal, and most live to tell about it. Most parents are not looking to terrorize young, untenured teachers and will be looking to work with you when it comes to the education of their children. Just remember that, unlike your students, they are not children and should be addressed in an appropriate manner.

6

CAMARADERIE, COMPETITION, CALUMNY, AND COFFEE TALK: THE POLITICS OF THE TEACHERS' LOUNGE

Oh, to have been there the day the wheel was invented. Try and imagine the looks on the faces of the cavepeople as they emerged from their dwellings to gaze upon this most awe-inspiring of miracles as it was rolled though the settlement's main thoroughfare. The inventor of said miracle no doubt stood proudly in the morning sunshine, her face beaming with pride as her now intellectually inferior neighbors moved cautiously forward for a closer look at her shining achievement. She had created something that would dramatically change their lives forever, and she was assuredly overcome with glee at the idea of it.

Now imagine the look on her face when her fellow citizens proceeded to smash her invention, her most modern of marvels, into tiny pieces with their clubs, as they sneered at her for daring to proffer such sacrilege to them. What prompted them to take such action against her gift that was so lovingly given? The answer is frighteningly simple. People are afraid of change. And teachers (who are supposedly some form of person) are the most frightened of all. Remember that little tidbit when you march into your new building armed with all of your brilliant ideas on the first day of school, for if you are not careful, you may notice some of the townspeople moving in your direction, and they will probably be dragging their clubs behind them.

Now that you have been thoroughly terrified, let's be serious. Most people are, at the very least, concerned when something new enters into their orderly, structured environment. That "something new" is you, and whether you like it or not, some of your new colleagues will be discussing you behind your back. This doesn't mean they will be overwhelmingly concerned with things like your taste in briefcases or how you dress. (Although, sadly, some will. Remember, high school never ends.) What they may be concerned with, at least initially, are the things that may affect their lives. Have you talked to the new guy yet? What's he like? Is he any better than that schmuck that got fired last year? Does he have a sense of humor? Can we curse in front of him?

These are some of the things that may concern your new loungemates. Granted, this kind of silliness no doubt goes on behind closed doors at many different types of workplaces, but you need to remember that the teacher is a strange animal. There is a special kind of routine that accompanies the job that you don't find in many others. In what other profession do you meet dozens of kids in the fall that you will guide on an intellectual journey that will tax your body and mind for forty weeks, which will then leave you exhausted both mentally and physically, prompting you to try and forget about it for two months just so you can turn around and start the process all over again in September? Not many, I assure you.

Teachers create very individualized routines to survive in this environment. For instance, some might enjoy cursing a blue streak in the teachers' lounge after a tough class to blow off steam. Will you, the newcomer, in this day of political correctness, pose a threat to that teacher's way of relaxing? Bear in mind, that teacher no doubt behaves that way in front of a group of people that he or she has come to know and trust over the years and who are not offended by his or her colorful speech. But now you have the same lunch period as Teacher X. How will you react when the F-bombs start hitting their targets?

TEACHERS AREN'T STUPID

Despite what every school-age kid in America will tell you, teachers are fairly intelligent. Well, most of them anyway. Before you develop a fear of walking into the teachers' lounge, bear in mind that the aforementioned Teacher X will probably not show off his potty mouth in front of you, at least not at first. What will happen, however, will be the feeling-out process, not unlike the ones the kids will put you through. It will no doubt begin with a slightly off-color comment here, an unflattering remark about a troublesome student there, and other things bordering on inappropriate in the workplace. Your job will be to communicate whether or not you care to listen to such things while you eat your tuna fish sandwich every day. And remember, it's okay to communicate "I'm not cool with that" if such talk offends you.

Remember, you are a professional working among other professionals and you should not have to put up with that. What we want to impress upon you, however, is to be tactful about how you communicate your response. The reason for this is that despite the fact that the champions of politically correct speech appear to have won that battle in public, there are still little pockets of resistance, people who enjoy saying things in private that would warrant a seven-second delay. Again, you don't have to hear it if you don't want to, but just be aware that you run the risk of being labeled "one of those people" if you object in the wrong way. And that may be fine with you, but if it's not, here are a few tips to help you communicate what you think is unacceptable and still allow you to make some friends along the way.

COMMON MISTAKES MADE BY NEW TEACHERS IN REGARD TO "POLITICALLY INCORRECT" COLLEAGUES

Laughing in Spite of the Fact That You Are Offended. Teacher X will try a few of his best jokes that will just barely scratch the surface of being unacceptable. If you ignore enough of them, he'll probably get the message and stop. Of course, if he doesn't, see the next bullet.

Not Speaking Up When Uncomfortable. There's nothing wrong with telling the armchair comedian that you think his subpar material is about what you'd expect from a teacher, but just think twice about how you say it. Phrasing your words with a little humor of your own wouldn't hurt either. This will tell him not only that you don't appreciate his comments, but that you are a clever one yourself, and will probably garner you some added respect.

Letting Things Get Out of Hand. Obviously, if a colleague's humor is something you find offensive in regard to your sex, race, or religion, you need to do something about it. If you don't feel comfortable talking to the offender, try asking a colleague you trust to pass on your feelings for you. If this fails, do not be afraid to ask a union representative to step in for you. If the behavior still continues, take it to the administration. And if that fails, call your attorney and start thinking about how you are going to spend all that settlement money.

Believing That if You Can't Beat 'Em, Join 'Em. As a new teacher who is looking to be taken seriously and accepted by your colleagues, do not feel you have to use foul language or share offensive jokes just because that seems to be the established tone of the teachers' lounge. Most school faculties consist of at least fifty people, and simply because you happen to have the same free period as some of the more "liberal" members, it does not mean that the entire staff behaves in such a way. You may be in for an unpleasant surprise when and if a more conservative member happens to join you and you have developed the lovely habit of offending people. Remember, trash talk that comes out of the mouths of twenty-year veteran teachers may seem funny and acceptable when they say it, but has a way of losing its charm when uttered by a newer, perhaps younger, teacher.

Of course, offensive language is only the tip of a very large iceberg in regard to teachers' lounge politics. You'll have to learn your school's customs when it comes to everything from how long it is acceptable to stay on the phone or occupy the computer to how much time you have to microwave your lunch. You'll find that you are constantly asking yourself foolish questions like, "Are those doughnuts for everybody? Am I supposed to replace the paper towels if I use the last one or do the custodians do that? She left the copy room, yet her school bag is actually still on line in front of me. Do I have to wait for her to come back or is it my turn to use the machine? Do we always sit at the same seats at lunch or is it first come, first served? Is it my responsibility to replace that ink cartridge?"

Trivial things like this may not seem like a big deal now, but just wait until you have that abandoned book bag staring you down in the copy room. These are the minutiae you will just have to figure out as you go. While each school has its own "rules" regarding these daily items, there is a universal political trap with which we can help, and that is the world of teachers' lounge gossip.

Every year our school hosts a basketball game between the faculty and the senior class, and every year the seniors win, simply because of the fact that the seniors are in the prime of life and the teachers are, well, you can probably imagine the shape they're in. Of course, if that competition were to be changed to a gossip contest, the teachers would demolish all that opposed them every year. Yes, even sixteen-year-old girls have nothing on a group of teachers when it comes to gossip.

Being new to a school is a lonely position to be in, and there is no faster way to feel like one of the guys (or gals) than to join in on a good gossip session. It serves two purposes: First, it usually makes someone, the subject of the chatter, look quite uncool, thereby making your coolness seem elevated in comparison. Second, it creates a bond among you and your conversationmates and makes it seem like you are becoming "in with the in crowd." Nevertheless, beware.

We don't know how many gossip sessions, be it one or two or ten or twenty, that one must participate in to gain the reputation of a gossip hound. One of the authors of this book has that very reputation, and has yet to shed it. When the whole faculty and administration get to a point where they don't trust you enough to discuss highly classified material with you, two bad things happen: First, you end up looking immature. Second, you miss out on the really good dirt. The good news is you can write a book about it!

If we are to remain realistic about this matter, we have to admit that everyone we know engages in a little bit of gossip, especially when among very trusted friends. That is human nature, and it is probably safe when you keep it within your established social circle. The problem with being a new teacher, though, is that you don't have an established social circle. Yes, you may have bonded with a few other rookies when together you successfully unjammed the copier or braved the cafeteria food. This does not mean you are "tight" enough with them to start bashing the other new guys, the old guys, or the bosses. In a year or two, if copy room bravado leads to beers at the local bar, which leads to calling each other on the weekends, which leads to summer barbeques, wedding invitations, and naming your children after each other, then you have found yourself a trusted gossip buddy. Until then, keep your thoughts to yourself.

COMMON MISTAKES MADE BY NEW TEACHERS IN REGARD TO GOSSIP

Trashing Anyone (Other Faculty, Students, or Administration) to People You Do Not Know Extremely Well. You are asking for trouble if you do this. While it is most likely true that you can trust your colleagues, you never know if the girl you trash with your buddy today will be best friends with said buddy the next day and turn around to trash you. In fact, we work with a woman who, when she was new, seemed awfully friendly with a particularly sleazy young member of our faculty. A group of us would go on and on about why he was not good enough for her, citing every reason from the fact that he was too chummy with the students to the fact that he never returned the favor when you paid for his drink at a bar. We *really* ripped him apart to her, and honest to God they ended up not only dating, but also getting married. Think we could have trusted her not to tell him what we said?

Venting about Students or Parents with Too Many People Around. There will come a time when you absolutely have to let off a little steam about parents or students who upset you. If your colleagues are like most of ours, they will be happy to listen and offer some good advice about how to handle things. However, it seems that every faculty (actually, every workplace in general) seems to have a saboteur. While that will be covered more extensively in the case studies, just be aware that some teachers who are looking to gain popularity will approach the student or parent with whom you are having trouble and try to win his or her favor by getting involved in your situation.

Going Off on a Tirade about the Administration for Every Little Thing. It is a guarantee that something your boss does will get on your nerves at some point. However, choose your complaining sessions wisely. It is true that faculties often have an "us vs. them" mentality, but nobody wants to hear you rant and rave every single time a policy is initiated. First and foremost, your fellow teachers will find it highly annoying. In addition, your opinions may find their way back to the administrative wing. If your school is anything like our school, some of the administrators were hired from "the outside," but some were promoted from within.

So that assistant principal who got under your skin by rearranging the fire drill system or awarding your parking spot to the kid who sold the most fund-raiser wrapping paper may have been sitting in your seat in the faculty lounge last year and may still be friends with the very people to whom you are complaining.

There are many other obvious political pitfalls of which you should be aware, like working to keep things highly professional if you decide, foolishly, to date another teacher. Of course, love is foolish by nature, so many of you will not be able to help it if that cute English teacher or hunky physical education teacher ends up being the one for you. We happen to work among a number of happy couples that began their courtship gazing over a tray of tater-tot surprise in the cafeteria, reaching for the same cheese Danish at faculty development, or giggling at all the same scenes in the state-required sexual harassment video. Nevertheless, try to keep things low-key until the relationship is in the later, more serious stages.

While faculty romance is certainly the brighter side of teacher politics, being part of a faculty can get ugly, and it gets no uglier than the dirty world of teacher competition. How can teachers help it? With all of the agencies out there, both local and national, who recognize individuals for great teaching, it is difficult not to desire the kudos for yourself, especially if your students are the judges.

Teachers in our school actually campaign, albeit jokingly, for the vote of favorite teacher each year. As much as chaperoning the prom is a long and often stressful night, teachers are secretly dying to do it because the seniors vote on which faculty members they want to share their special night with and it feels good to know that you are one of them. And, when it comes to the competitive world of electives, we would be lying if we said that students didn't choose their classes based partially on subject interest, and partially according to the popularity of the teacher running the show.

COMMON MISTAKES MADE BY NEW TEACHERS IN REGARD TO TEACHER COMPETITION

Trying Too Hard to Be the "Cool Teacher" During Your First Few Years. In the beginning, it is best to simply try to be a great teacher as opposed to being a cool teacher. As you gain comfort and build a good reputation, the coolness will follow as you will know more students in the building and be able to come out of your shell a bit more. Each year, more and more of your personality and sense of humor will shine through and soon the kids will be hanging around and joking with you after school the way they do with some of your veteran colleagues.

Taking On Too Many Activities. There is no faster track to a cool reputation and a better paycheck than to load up on the coaching and club leading. While that is something you should definitely try to get involved in during your first year, keep it to a minimum. If you are coaching, which any coach will tell you is a full-time job of its own, pass on the offer to moderate the Junior Birdwatchers of America Club. While getting involved is as good a way for you to get to know people as it is for the students, you have to be ready to commit to your own students and students involved in your club. Spreading yourself too thin will only backfire and lead to a decline in popularity and a reputation for being undependable.

Talking Negatively about Another Teacher with Students, Even if You Think That Teacher Deserves It. You will overhear a great deal of chatter from your students about other teachers, and it is very tempting to get involved in what they are saying. If you hear them going off on one of your colleagues, interrupt them and say that you would appreciate it if they did not talk that way about another teacher in front of you. If they start to whine about the injustices they have suffered at the hands of that teacher, stop them even if you agree that the teacher was unfair. You never know how exaggerated their stories are, and you never know what they plan to say about you when they enter their next class!

"Campaigning" in Order to Get Students to Request You as a Teacher or to Take an Elective You Are Teaching. Every year we have an "electives fair" where teachers set up a table during lunch periods to answer questions about the electives they teach so the students can choose an appropriate class. If your school does the same, avoid telling students how bored they will be if they choose another colleague's class over yours. While there are teachers who will absolutely use such tactics to fill their classrooms, it is tacky and unfair to the students and your colleagues. Listen to the student express his or her needs and base your recommendation on that, not your quest to impress your bosses with an overfilled roster.

CASE STUDIES

Case One: Beware of Saboteurs

The need to be well liked and popular is a natural instinct in humans (just ask Willy Loman), yet it is one they should try desperately to ignore if they choose to become teachers. It is not that having the students "like you" is a bad thing; it is just that making it your priority will backfire. It is a fact that most students will like you if you treat them fairly, take the time to talk to them about your subject or whatever other appropriate subjects happen to be on their minds, and are basically pleasant to be around.

While I am sure most of you work on faculties (like I do) where the majority of the staff members fit that description, there always seems to be one who is miserable to be there and has a problem with almost every kid he teaches and teacher with whom he works. I know one of those, and as a new teacher working with him, I was a political disaster waiting to happen.

In all fairness, I had been warned. There were stories about him, there was a "hostile work environment" lawsuit I had heard something about, and I was gently warned by other teachers to stay out of his way and to tell the administration or a union representative if something went wrong. Unfortunately, he worked in my department and avoiding him completely was impossible. I have to say that I was not naive enough nor did I have the desire to actually trust or befriend him, but I was not as careful as I should have been and I paid the price.

My first warning sign that he was a bit of a shady character was when I returned to work after having my appendix out. He was walking by my classroom full of tenth graders when he stuck his lecherous head in and asked me, in front of my class, if "the thong days were over" now that I had an appendectomy scar. I know what you're thinking, that an appendectomy scar and the wearing of a thong have nothing to do with each other and you are right. And no, he had no way of knowing about my undergarment habits. He was merely making an assumption. But we were dealing with a real nutty one here, so that kind of inappropriate and wacky comment was commonplace.

Not wanting to be part of a mounting, preexisting, legally complex problem during my first year of teaching, I decided to let the thong thing slide (I mean that figuratively) and I kept it to myself and endured great suffering at the hands of my imaginative tenth graders in the meantime. I didn't want to run to the administration like a damsel in distress, I didn't want them to think I was prancing around the school discussing my choice of underpants, I didn't want to look like I was starting trouble, and most of all I did not want to get subpoenaed. Basically, I was a big, appendixless wimp.

A few weeks passed and it was time for English students throughout the school to embark on their favorite journey of all, the writing of the grade-level research paper. While this task is daunting enough for teachers and students alike, it became even more stressful for me when I discovered that the only free library time included class periods that had to be shared with Mr. Thong.

While this went directly against my vow to avoid him, it also presented two other dangers. One, it would immediately remind the class (especially the male members) of the controversial comment and I would have to hear about it all over again when we were sharing library space. Second, Mr. Thong was erroneously under the impression that he was King of the Research Paper and would undoubtedly try to drum up business for his writing electives that no one ever wanted to take (because of his character) and would also have a number of criticisms about my method of teaching research. While a smart person would have waited until Mr. Thong's class was done with their writing unit and sign up for library time later, it was getting late in the year and I did not want my classes to start a project of this magnitude in May or June.

So off we went to the library where Mr. Thong's class was researching away, and we joined them and actually coexisted quite peacefully for the first day. Yes, there were rumblings about him being the guy who made the thong comment, but in all honesty the class (after laughing for weeks about it) actually saw just how offensive the comment was and began referring to him as "that perverted guy." Even though I should have, I did not correct them.

As the day ended, I was under the impression that things had gone quite well when Mr. Thong approached me. He asked me how I thought my teaching of research was going, and in the spirit of keeping my distance from him, I simply answered, "Fine." He responded by saying that he was a real expert in research writing and that he had a few tips if I was interested. Now, being a desperate new teacher I would normally have devoured tips on writing from any of my brilliant veteran colleagues from the English Department. Unfortunately, I really wanted to keep my involvement with this particular colleague to a minimum so I told him I was quite pleased with the methods I was already using. Apparently, my answer was fodder for his campaign to destroy my credibility with my classes.

The next day in the library, I noticed that Mr. Thong was paying very little attention to his own students. While that was not unusual, I noticed something that was: He was going from table to table of my students, attempting to teach *them* how to write a research paper. I overheard him saying things like, "She has no idea how to teach writing" and "Do it her way for now, but take my class next year and you'll really learn how to do this." My students, thankfully, simply thought he was weird and did not see his comments as the answer to their research prayers. I'd like to think it was their loyalty to me; however, it was more likely that learning how to write a research paper was not the top priority in their lives.

I ignored his behavior for a little while. However, after a couple of days it became a real distraction. His students were off the wall because no one was monitoring them, and my students could not so much as open a book without Mr. Thong hovering over them to see if they were writing their bibliography cards out the way he preferred. I approached him, and he said he was doing this to make sure that they learned the right way and that he was just trying to make my job easier. I asked him to stop, and he did not.

I did not know what to do (well, I knew, I just did not feel like getting the union or the administration involved), so I did what anyone would do and bitched about the situation behind the guy's back at lunch. I let it all spill out, the comment about the thong days, the offer to teach me how to teach writing, and the comments that he was making to my students. My buddies in the English Department went crazy. They were appalled that I had let this go on the way I had, and they emphasized the importance of getting some kind of authority involved. While I agreed to have a sort of "peer mediation" with him with a union representative present, I refused to involve the administration so as not to look like a troublemaker.

We had our little meeting, and the representative urged me to bring the case to the administration, but I never did. We decided that being in the library together simply could not happen, so we went on alternating days for the remainder of our projects. To this day, though, there is a certain amount of tension between us (actually, the tension seems to exist between him and pretty much the rest of the faculty), but we tend to coexist without incident. Unfortunately, other new teachers have found themselves in almost identical situations, and had I been a little more assertive I might have saved them the anxiety that I endured.

Case Two: The Strange Case of the Elusive Elective

It was in the autumn of 1996 when I again found myself attending to the education of children at the high school level. Having made good my escape from a Bronx junior high some two months earlier, I was looking forward to forgetting that terrifying experience and allowing myself to become assimilated among my newest colleagues, far from the din that had plagued me so terribly the previous year. Unfortunately, the relative calm with which I was greeted in the borough of Queens was soon to be interrupted by a new type of unpleasantness, one so dastardly and insidious that I did not even notice it until it was too late.

The atmosphere surrounding my new teaching situation was indescribable those first few days. Granted, any change in situation from the one I had just abandoned would have easily been seen as an improvement, and as I would learn later, this new school certainly had its share of problems, but I still spent the beginning of that school year feeling as if I were gracing the halls of some aged Ivy League university (relatively speaking, of course). This was a fact that did not go unnoticed by my fellow faculty members. One in particular, whose kindness and generosity were matched only by her eloquence, remarked, "So, Chris, how are the little bastards treating you?"

"You know, Agnes, if you had met some of the kids from my previous school, you might not call these kids bastards anymore."

"Don't worry, rookie, in a few months your feeling of bliss from getting your transfer here will wear off and you'll see these kids for what they really are."

Now, technically, I was not a rookie. I had just survived ten months in the steaming cauldron of misery that is junior high school and lived to tell the tale, but I did not bother to point that fact out to Agnes, who seemed to have already made up her mind about a lot of facts already. Instead, I attempted to steer the conversation away from verbally assaulting children to one I was more interested in, the subject of teaching: "Well, I guess time will tell. I'm just glad to be getting away from doing crowd control and getting back to some real teaching again."

"Wow, it really sounds like you had a hard time up there. Didn't you get a chance to teach anything fun?"

I fought hard to suppress the urge to burst into hysterics at this inane, uninformed comment. Instead, I attempted to respond with the same sort of verve that Agnes injected into her conversation: "No."

"Well, you should ask Trudy at the next department meeting to let you teach one of our senior electives next year. You'd probably enjoy it."

As many of us have learned the hard way, all new teachers must be prepared to receive the class assignments that have been previously turned down by the existing faculty. I was no exception. My schedule consisted of five periods of freshman English so overcrowded that I had to hope that students would be absent in order for each child to have a desk to sit and work at. Bearing that in mind, and understanding that I was the lowest man on the proverbial totem pole, try and imagine the joy that suddenly coursed through me at the very mention of my teaching one of the most coveted of classes, the Holy Grails of English, the senior electives!

These were not your run-of-the-mill courses, no sir, they focused on things like psychology, great women writers, mystery, science fiction, and, dare I say it, *film study*! Could it be that easy? Simply raise my hand and ask Trudy, our department chair, to grant me one of those sacred cows? That's how it sounded coming from Agnes, but as I should have realized, having actually spoken to Agnes on more than one occasion, what she said and what she truly believed about things did not always align.

I looked forward to that next department meeting like a child looks forward to Christmas. The days dragged on and on, and yet I always made sure to be on my best behavior, just in case Trudy was checking on me through her magic telescope to see if I were being naughty or nice. Finally, the day came. I was early, of course, to make sure my seat in the semicircle of desks was in just the right place for Trudy to be able to look me in the face without her having to strain her neck when I asked the big question.

Eventually, the rest of the department showed up and the meeting got under way. I fought hard to concentrate on the mundane topics on the agenda, exciting things like the scoring of the new Regents exam and how we needed to be more vigilant in collecting books from our students. After what seemed like an eternity, all of the agenda items had been addressed and Trudy asked if anyone had any other business they wanted to bring up.

My hand shot into the air, an act that startled my fellow educators, already getting up from their desks, who had apparently never asked a question at a department meeting before. They reluctantly sat back down, an act that should have warned me about the reception my upcoming comments were about to elicit. Blind to this nonverbal warning, I proudly gave voice to the request that had buoyed me over the past few weeks: "Trudy, I'd like to volunteer to teach a senior elective next year."

Trudy's countenance changed in a strange way after hearing my request. She looked like a person who had just received some mildly bad news, like her parking meter had expired and her car had been towed away or her fish had all passed away because she hadn't been treating the water in her tank properly. She looked at me that way for a moment, and then took a quick glance around the room before responding, "Really? Which one did you have in mind?"

I suddenly felt like the idiot at a party that gets so drunk that he ends up knocking over the buffet table or breaking the stereo and ruining all the fun for everyone else. Colleagues who had hardly noticed me before were now leaning toward one another and whispering, in not-so-hushed tones: "What's this kid's name again?" "How long has he been teaching?" "Isn't he new? Who does he think he is?" "He had better not be talking about my class. I created the damn thing!" That last comment came from none other than Agnes herself.

Defeated, I forced out the closest thing to a face-saving remark I could think of: "Well, anything that might be available."

At this, the man who taught the film class spoke up: "Is anybody here interested in giving up an elective next year?"

As if on cue, the gentleman who taught psychology chimed right in: "Well, I was thinking of giving up the psychology course, but then I'd need to have my head examined!"

This final comment was met with what sounded like a rehearsed chuckle, as if this wasn't the first time they had teamed up to protect their most sacred of territory. Mercifully, Trudy put an end to it all: "Chris, why don't you stop by my office later and we can discuss the department's policy on the rotation of electives, okay? And as for the rest of you, unless there are any other questions . . . "

There were no other questions. Everyone left in better spirits than when they came in. I did not go to Trudy's office to discuss the department's rotation policy. Regardless of whatever she might have told me, I knew that the only way I would have a shot at one of those classes would have to involve either the retirement or death of one of the elective teachers. Instead, I went home and thought of creative ways to arrange my classroom to accommodate the increased number of freshman.

Case Three: Union Jacks

In the spirit of self-analysis, I am embarrassed to say that my greatest weakness my first few years (although I would not have admitted it during an interview) was immaturity. My clothes were too young, my attitude was too whimsical, and my sense of humor was still appropriate for the dorm room I had inhabited a mere three months before starting my job. Nevertheless, I managed to exist in a very adult world without getting fired, which is still a mystery. With this unfortunate immaturity came its likely companion, naiveté. This particular, not-so-cute trait landed me in an awkward political predicament.

The first year I taught there was a great deal of change occurring in my building. The principal, assistant principal, and superintendent were all in their last year, and we were, at the time, working without a contract. People were very upset and nervous about such conditions; however, I personally did not see the urgency of the situation. Looking back, I can see how stressful it really was. But back then I did not know the first thing about unions and contracts and how crucial they were.

Union elections were coming up, and there were rumblings about certain people running for president. I did not know many people in the building, but I did know our union president from all of the new teacher meetings. She was amazing: well-spoken, fair, concerned, and *highly* respected by faculty, staff, administration, and the district leaders. Not only had I planned on voting for her, I could not imagine why anyone else would even run, especially when so much seemed to be at stake.

One afternoon while I was sitting at my hall duty post, two young male teachers, both named John, came up for what I assumed was an innocent chat. We talked about how my year was going and we had the usual conversation about that, but then things got a little weird. They began asking me about the leadership in the building. Questions like: Did I feel that the current union officials had my best interest, as a new teacher, in mind? Didn't it seem like the current union officials were more concerned with retirement buy-outs than with protecting the untenured staff? Didn't I think that coaching stipends, which were traditionally earned by younger staff members, were crappy and that no one was doing anything about it?

Taken back a bit, I answered with the traditional reply of the immature: "I *guess* so." They smiled and said that they were happy to see that I was on their side, that they knew they could count on me, and that they knew I hung around with all of the new hires and that they would appreciate my using my charming personality to get the message out that they were planning on running against the current president so that there would finally be some equity around here. Naive little thing that I was, I didn't think anything of it.

Weeks later, with elections pending, I noticed how tense things were getting around the building and in the faculty workroom. People were upset about the Johns running for president and vice president. I would listen to my faculty buddies (both old and young) voice concerns that fairly new teachers with specific agendas weren't really the appropriate choice right now, with a new superintendent arriving and contract negotiations approaching. Foolishly, I decided to chime in.

"Well," I said, "maybe it is time for someone who cares more about coaching stipends than retirement benefits." At this statement, I got the room's attention. "Also," I continued as I spooned the chocolate pudding snack pack my roommate had packed for me in my lunch into my moving mouth, "maybe it is time that someone with the welfare of new teachers in mind took office."

As I continued, I realized that the majority of the room's population was looking at me quizzically. When I asked them what was going on, they asked me how someone who had been at the school for one month came to these conclusions about union officials I had just met. They wanted to know if I was aware of how far we had come as a staff in regard to salary, benefits, retirement, and yes, coaching, all because of the thousands of hours of work the current president dedicated to negotiating the last contract. Sinking into my seat, I said I was not. When they asked where I had heard such things, I quickly blurted out that that was what the Johns had told me, and that they wanted me to let all of the new teachers know how much better things would be if they were elected.

While the mirror tells me that I could never be known as the face that launched a thousand ships, my mouth sure was highly capable in that area. The Johns found themselves quite unpopular, not for wanting change but for their slimy tactics that involved lying about the accomplishments and intentions of someone who had worked unbelievably hard for the good of the entire staff, and using innocent new teachers like me to do their dirty work.

Thankfully, the current president was reelected and the contract negotiations worked out well. I don't think I'm the Johns' favorite person, but at least I am working under the best conditions possible, thanks to our union representatives of that year.

ADMINISTRATIVE ANALYSIS

Case One

Amy really made a major mistake here, and it was not following instructions to let the administration know if there were any incidents with, as she calls him, Mr. Thong. The mistake was serious on two levels. First, Amy's reputation was at stake with the first incident. I am sure many students and parents heard about the "thong," comment, and although she was not at fault for what happened, it certainly did not make her look good to remain silent. News of the comment never made its way down to the administrative annex, but if it had and it had come from any source but Amy herself, she would have had some interesting questions to answer. This does not in any way diminish the fact that she was an obvious victim of sexual harassment, which leads us to the second point.

Unfortunately, people in the workplace with repulsive tendencies like "Mr. Thong" occasionally, and I implore you to pardon the pun, slip through the cracks and must be rooted out by their coworkers. Ignoring a poorly chosen comment from a colleague who may be having an off day is one thing; allowing a verbal assault from a person who should clearly not be teaching children is another.

Case Two

This case is both simple and complex at the same time. Quite often, particularly with secondary-level electives, you do find the same people teaching the same things year after year. New teachers, eager to make friends, don't tend to "rock the boat" and are often content to accept the "less glamorous" assignments. This is exactly what Chris did. He let his fear of stepping on toes prevent him from learning how to request a class he would no doubt have brought a lot of enthusiasm and freshness to. So, on the one hand, you have a complex situation for the new teacher who doesn't want to make waves. On the other hand, we need to remember that teachers are not employed to find the most comfortable niche they possibly can for themselves; they are there to do the best job they can to educate kids.

As far as I am concerned, there is no such thing as a "sacred cow" when it comes to teaching. Chris's mistake was not taking his department head's advice to meet with her and discuss the school's policy on rotation. There is no reason in the world why a new teacher should feel excluded from teaching something they are passionate about. You can take excuses like "Well, Mr. So-and-So has been teaching it for twenty years and really knows what he's doing" or "She created the class and deserves to teach it" and throw them out the window. Chris didn't want to make any enemies so he deferred to the veterans in his department that basically bullied him into submission. Are those the type of people you should be worried about losing as friends? I don't think so.

If you find yourself in a similar situation and don't mind upsetting the carefully constructed universes of a few people that probably wouldn't bother with you anyway, talk to your department head and find out how to request a class. If you feel like you are not being helped at that level, go to your principal. Just don't let yourself be intimidated by someone with gray hair and more years on the job than you.

Case Three

Amy is right about the root of this problem, and it was immaturity and inexperience. Her age got the better of her. She had just come from college, where little gossip scandals may have been an everyday occurrence and students spent more time discussing them than they did going to class. The problem was that this was not college: It was the workplace, and there was much more at stake. The smartest thing to have done would have been to politely excuse herself from speaking with the Johns and to have sought a trusted, more experienced colleague from which to get the real story on past negotiations. Of course, she could also have obtained a copy of her contract and read it for herself.

The real offenders here were the Johns, and new teachers have to be careful that they do not become the center of faculty scandal gossip *ever* if possible, but certainly not during their untenured years. Keeping your wits about you and staying out of situations that seem unsavory during the first few years is crucial to building a good, respectable reputation.

FINAL TIPS ON TEACHER POLITICS

As we have tried to point out above, teachers, just like all adults, retain quite a bit of their adolescent selves when they grow up. As a result, they will quite often act like adolescents, and that is not a bad thing. The problems arise when adults forget when it is and is not appropriate to engage in such behavior. And, like children, adults don't like it when others try to impose limitations on what they can and can't do. The job of the new teacher is to communicate what he or she is comfortable with when the cavepeople come out of their dwellings to size up the new arrival. With a little tact and subtlety, you will soon be the best of cavemates. Don't let the people with the clubs scare you. They were just like you once.

7

AND IN THIS CORNER . . . SCHOOL VIOLENCE AND THE NEW TEACHER

Regardless of whatever technological innovations occur in our lifetimes and despite any advances made toward uniting our world, one thing will always remain true: People will find something to fight about. Whether it be a friendly disagreement over the interpretation of a piece of poetry or two middle-aged men punching it out at a supermarket over a parking spot, conflicts between people will always be a constant. While conflict is not necessarily a bad thing, it is the severity of these conflicts and the choices people make in resolving them that cause all the problems. Naturally, school-age children are just as prone to conflict as adults are, and the level and severity of the conflicts can range from downright silly to gut-wrenchingly tragic. Let us begin with an observation of the male animal.

When people hear "school fight," they quite often assume that the altercation has taken place between two males. Let us set the record straight: Young women, when sufficiently provoked, can be just as vicious as any boy, and there will probably be just as many girl fights as boy ones. The first thing to remember is that they all need to be dealt with. Obviously, two kids beating the hell out of each other need to not only be stopped but must also be held accountable.

Of course, not all altercations will be this severe. Quite often you will encounter small stuff like kids playfully pushing each other in the hall. Well, the bottom line is that someone could get hurt, even in an incident as benign as this. So how severe a punishment should these hormonally charged young men receive? A passing adult telling them to break it up and standing there until they do is just fine. You could issue harsher punishments, but then you'd have lines of kids wrapped around the building waiting for sentence to be passed down, a major drain on school resources. Let's break down the different types of battles you will encounter, and where you will most likely encounter them.

GOTTA CATCH 'EM ALL!

First and foremost, you have your little guys. They tend to find themselves in minor, almost laughable skirmishes where the participants usually wind up pulling each other's hair and crying by the time it is over. Come back in twenty minutes and they are probably best friends again. These irritating little slap-fests are usually over such minutiae as missing baseball cards, stepping on someone's foot, or, dare I say it, spilt milk. It doesn't take much to break these up. Again, with smaller kids, the very mention of going to the principal's office will speed the healing process between the two combatants and the odds of a rematch are pretty slim.

BETWEEN PUBERTY AND POKÉMON CARDS

Once they get to middle school age, the tactics tend to change somewhat. It is here that, for the guys anyway, strange things start to happen. Unpleasant odors begin to emanate from the armpit, something resembling hair begins to sprout up on the upper lip, and what was once a lovely alto or soprano voice suddenly morphs into an almost indistinguishable series of grunts. And, as this most painful of transformations begins to take place, so too does a transformation in the young male's way of thinking. Rushing home to watch cartoons suddenly doesn't seem as important anymore. The urge to play with those most masculine of toys, action figures, is mysteriously replaced by a desire to blow them up with fireworks. And, even more frightening, is a sudden interest in fashion.

The little boys that were so cute and cuddly in elementary school are becoming little men, and cute and cuddly are not descriptions they want to be associated with. And, of course, there is the blossoming interest in females. Yes, they've always been around, but when did they start looking and smelling so good? These are the questions the pubescent male ponders. And as he attempts to decipher the female riddle, he tends to take out his frustrations in other ways, mostly physical.

The relatively innocent roughhousing they did as boys starts to become a little more intense. Bullying, which by all means existed at the elementary level, becomes more hurtful, in both the physical and mental sense. Cliques develop, and the level of physical development of the members generally determines membership. When is the last time you saw a *Star Wars* geek in the school weight room? How many athletes do you think meet up on Monday morning to talk about whether Starbuck and Apollo will hook up on *Battlestar Galactica*? Certainly there must be exceptions that prove the rule, so allow me to be the first to wish you good luck in finding them. Fights among these kids tend to be exhibitions of power: I'm taller and have bigger muscles than you so I'm going to beat your ass in front of my friends and have them look up to me. And if you put up any kind of a fight, I have my boys here to ensure that you are humiliated anyway. Once again, folks, take it from people who know.

These battles, if they are still going on by the time an adult shows up, will need your intervention, which will probably consist of you pulling the bigger boy off of the smaller one and suppressing the sorrow you feel for him as the crowd of kids that has no doubt gathered around him points and laughs. Obviously, they both need to be reported to an administrator to determine what happened. Hopefully, to coin a phrase, the punishment(s) will fit the crime(s).

HIGHWAY TO HELL

Finally, we make it to the big stage: high school. Countless hours of television have been devoted to the exciting lives of the gorgeous children who grace high school halls. Strangely enough, the actors playing the students never appear to be age-appropriate. They might look like college seniors, but not high school freshmen. And, each week, one of our heroes suddenly has a new obstacle to overcome, to draw attention to a typical "teen problem." Thankfully, the end of the episode usually clears them up. Dylan crashed the Porsche! What will his father say? Brenda drank half a beer and puked all over her brother! Who will think she's pretty now?

While some attention given to actual problems teenagers face is better than no attention at all, let it be said that these programs do not paint a true portrait of American high school life. The fact is that in the real world these problems occur on a daily basis, with greater intensity, and in much greater numbers. Now, depending on where you live and teach, you may think these shows are representative of true fact. Certainly there are well-to-do areas where attractive children drive expensive cars and have lavish parties overflowing with alcohol and worse. What we need to ask ourselves is, Why? To be cool? Of course. To fit in? Absolutely.

But let us not forget the mind-set: They do these things because they are fun and allow them to rebel, and they do them everywhere. One group's finished basement is another group's park bench. They make do with what they have. And the latest thing they have to deal with is the idea that they are becoming adults, a fact that is absolutely true and cannot be ignored. They want to do adult things. They want to drink, drive (unfortunately at the same time), curse, smoke whatever they can get their hands on, and, yes, they want to have sex. They want to experiment. They want to be adults, even though they are not, at least not quite yet. Parents have heard the patented responses: "You know you did it when you were my age!" And they're right. But once again, parents have more experience. Of course, that makes no difference, because teenagers know everything.

Why is all this time being spent on a return visit to the teen mind-set? Simply put, you need to understand why kids do the things they do. By the time they reach high school, they think they have it all figured out. They've got girlfriends and jobs and a disappearing curfew and college plans and all sorts of things that make them feel independent. The problem is they're still stuck in a system more structured for kids several years their junior. Cram a few thousand kids with a few thousand different agendas into the same building and sparks are going to fly. If a young man sees someone he already doesn't like talking to his girlfriend, a girl he may feel is his property (I know, I know, those guys are jerks), he's going to get angry. He's going to want to take matters into his own hands, so to speak. Talking it out is probably not on his "How to Get Things Done" list.

Remember that physical development so eloquently detailed a few paragraphs back? Rest assured it has continued. And the threat of going to the principal's office is about as effective a deterrent as flicking the lights on and off or blowing a whistle; they don't even register. That's where the real problem for the teacher develops.

The student doesn't see you standing on the sidelines waving your arms about and saying what a great kid you are and please don't do this. All they see is the threat, the threat to their adult world, and they want it taken out. God help you if you get in the way.

TIPS FOR NEW (AND OLD) TEACHERS IN REGARD TO HANDLING VIOLENCE

One of the many problems with school violence is that there really is no good way to handle it. The situations are so unpredictable and potentially dangerous that even the most seasoned of veterans may have trouble deciding what to do when an incident erupts. Even so, it's your responsibility to get involved. Just how you get involved depends on a variety of factors. Should a pregnant woman behave exactly the same way as one of her colleagues in this situation? The answer is absolutely not, for she is already tasked with defending the life inside of her. Of course, that doesn't mean she should ignore the situation and run in the opposite direction either. Believe it or not, there are plenty of things a teacher can do to not only stop these conflicts when they occur, but to stop them before they start as well.

Call for Backup. Scream and holler. Earlier, we suggested that there might be some individuals so determined to enter into battle that any protests you voiced would be ignored. While that may be true in some cases, it is not true for all. After all, kids have had teachers telling them what to do their whole lives. They may instinctively respond when given a direction, particularly if the teacher knows one of their names. If that doesn't have an impact on the combatants, it will most certainly empty every classroom within earshot and you will soon have a plethora of people coming to your aid. Just make sure that someone gets security, as a two-person fistfight can turn quickly into a forty-student rumble.

Get Close, But Not Too Close. Oftentimes you can stop a fight with words if you get there at just the right moment, particularly before those involved get too caught up in the emotion of the event. A highly visible authority figure is an excellent deterrent. Being in close proximity also allows you to analyze those involved in the conflict and help you to answer the following questions: Does one child seem more intent on doing this than the other? Does it appear either of them has a weapon of some kind? Which child should I grab in order to stop this thing from getting any worse? Of course, in the heat of battle, the line between student and teacher can become blurred, so be careful not to present yourself as an even greater threat to the two people already charged with emotion. Keep your distance, but bear in mind, as much as you loathe the idea, you may have to put your hands on one or the both of them.

Keep Your Eyes Open. If you are not one of the people directly involved in physically breaking up a fight, get your head together and watch very carefully. You will want to be able to provide an accurate account of the event if students claim teachers hurt them while separating them from the violence. Your word will go a long way. You will also want to keep a close eye on the kids in the crowd. Occasionally, a student on the sidelines might try to throw in a cheap shot or worse, so if you aren't able to stop it, you can at least identify the guilty party.

Be Prepared to Go All the Way. This is the question everyone dreads: When do I put my hands on a child? Well, as the adult in the area of the conflict, you have a responsibility to do whatever you can to stop these kids from hurting each other. Underline "whatever you can." If you are physically unable to break up a fight, don't try to.

The idea here is to reduce the chance of injury, not increase it. If, on the other hand, you feel confident that by intervening you are not taking your own life into your hands and you have tried every other method available to you, it is appropriate to get between the combatants. Some people worry about the legal ramifications about touching a student under any circumstance and would rather do nothing in one of these situations. Well, guess what, it's your job to get involved. Remember, do whatever you physically can. It's doing nothing that can get you into trouble.

That Goes Double for a "Chick Fight." When the girls brawl, you have to be extra careful no matter what gender you are. While most people think that male teachers are at a natural risk when breaking up a girl fight, female teachers need to be just as careful.

We don't know why, but when young girls get into a fight, they automatically think that everyone trying to separate them is really trying to "cop a feel." Really, it is a defense mechanism. They know that if they are pulled away by a male teacher and they scream, "Stop touching my . . ." that teacher will drop them like a hot coal. They have a similar strategy with the female teachers, where they enjoy questioning that teacher's sexual orientation at the top of their lungs, which is not as effective as accusing the male teachers of being perverts, but it does make the situation a bit more uncomfortable. Therefore, when the ladies are having it out, be extra careful when separating them.

Keep It Together. Witnessing a live brawl can be frightening, dramatic, and emotional, and sometimes the adults involved react in a similar fashion. While it is definitely unnerving, you need to act matter-of-factly until you are in the privacy of your car, or at least the faculty bathroom. Until then, falling apart is inappropriate, distracting, and annoying.

Get Over Yourself. Once things have settled down and you go back to your classes, your students are going to want to talk all about the excitement that ensued, primarily focusing on your heroics. If your adrenaline high is still intact, you might want to go over every detail with your admiring audience of young people. All we can say is, don't do it, and that is more easily said than done. You never know what will end up happening *legally* in regard to the fight, and it is best to play down your involvement and the incident itself with your students. Nevertheless, your faculty buddies will want to hear all about it after the bell rings, so let them take you out for a beer after work if you feel the need to brag about your involvement. But remember, keep your voice down when in public! You never know who is listening!

CASE STUDIES

Case One: The Hero

I once broke up a fight that resulted in me cutting my hand (on, of all things, the I.D. card hanging around my neck). The wound was really not bad at all, but my colleagues insisted I go down and see the school nurse. As I arrived, I noticed that the police officer assigned to our school was already there interviewing one of the combatants. After he was finished and I had received my oversized Band-Aid, he approached me and asked what transpired between the two individuals.

I explained how I observed the two squaring off against each other, spouting obscenities and waiting for one or the other to make the first move. I shouted at the boys to break it up but was ignored. It was going to happen whether I liked it or not. I got closer to them, but not too close, fearing that I might be considered a threat, and basically waited for one of them to throw a punch. It came a fraction of a second later. After the first boy, clearly the aggressor, started landing punches, I immediately grabbed him around the midsection, pulled him off of the other boy, and, with his arms flailing about, pushed him up against the wall.

All thoughts of a thankful victim rushing off to get an administrator quickly died when the second boy proceeded to throw himself up against me and hurl punches *around* me, landing several on his enemy before the cacophony led to classrooms emptying and additional teachers coming to my aid. After I finished delivering my report to the officer, I couldn't resist the temptation to ask in my usual sarcastic, carefree manner: "I guess I'll probably get sued for grabbing that kid, huh?"

What the officer said next really stuck with me: "Well, buddy, all I can say is that if it was my kid, I'd be thankful to know that the teachers in the building were ready to step in and keep him from really getting hurt."

After that, the idea of teacher-as-referee made more sense. Before this incident, I was hesitant to get in between two brawlers. After speaking with the officer, I suddenly realized what should have been obvious. It all goes back to the mind-set. I was the closest adult. The buck stopped with me. There was no costumed hero around to save the day, just me.

Case Two: Know What You're Getting Into

Isn't Chris so tough? Well, I wish I were as brave as he was, but that simply is not the case. Even so, I have witnessed my share of little "spats" between both boys and girls that turned physical and reached varying levels of severity. Of course, some were more difficult to watch than others. One burning example for me involved a girl I was very fond of, a foster child who was having an extremely difficult time fitting in at school. The children teased her mercilessly for not coming from a "normal" home. One afternoon, she ended up tangling with a few of the "tougher" girls in the school. I actually helped break it up by pulling her out of the mix (after about five other teachers began the process of separating the girls), and the only thing that helped calm her down was the fact that a familiar, trusted person was there to listen to her side of the story and help her get herself together. In that situation, I was fortunate to have been dealing with a student with whom I had had time to build a relationship. When I first started teaching, however, I was not so lucky.

I did witness one fight get out of control, and it was during my student teaching semester. I was assigned a class of remedial seniors, and my cooperating teacher thought it would be appropriate to leave me alone with them on my second day.

I had two problems going into this situation. First, my middle school student teaching experience was in a fantastic school with one of the most amazing teachers I have ever met. She certainly let me take control of the class, but she waited until I was there for a number of weeks before she did so. I was used to her professionalism and guidance, and I expected it at the next placement, but I was mistaken. The second problem was my age and appearance. I was only twenty-one, and I was wearing this geeky, flowery, *Little House on the Prairie*-type dress that made me look like I was about twelve. I don't even have an excuse about the outfit. It was 1998 and I should have known better.

Anyway, although it was mid–school year for the students, it was my first week and my cooperating teacher had understandably had it with these kids. They were pretty unruly right from the start of the class, and I did not even know their names, so it was impossible to deal with them. I began to feel sorry for every substitute teacher in the universe who must feel like this on a daily basis.

Eventually, the students started asking me general questions about my life and I decided to answer a few. Then, out of nowhere, this one student yelled out that I was the skinniest teacher they had ever had. I said thank you, and tried to move the class on. Then, some other student reminded him that they had had a skinnier teacher last year. The first student told him how stupid he was for thinking that, and they began to beat each other, first with fists, and then with desks.

I had absolutely no idea what to do. I was not an employee of the district, and my cooperating teacher had not explained a procedure for this type of event. I thought for a second about breaking them up, and realized I had no chance.

Soon, other boys were getting involved, bulletin boards were being ripped down, and girls were screaming for me to get security. How did I do that? The school was huge, and I had no idea where to go. I asked one of the girls to go, and she told me to use the phone. I had not noticed the phone before, and the idea sounded great but I did not know the security code and it was not written down anywhere that I knew of. Luckily, we were causing enough of a racket that other teachers (all except my cooperating teacher) came in and they had called security. Embarrassingly, they all kept asking the class, including me, where the teacher was. I explained that I was the student teacher, and they found it slightly amusing. In the end I did not get in trouble, but I was the last student teacher my college ever placed with that cooperating teacher.

ADMINISTRATIVE ANALYSIS

Case One

Overall, Chris did fairly well in a very difficult situation, but he might have bitten off a little more than he could chew. Breaking up a fight is never a pleasant thing, particularly when you stumble upon one alone like Chris did. Remember that the fight came to an abrupt end when the noise level increased so much that the teachers in the nearby classrooms heard it and rushed out to help. If Chris had managed to alert the teachers in the area when he first arrived on the scene, the outcome may have been different. Granted, walking around a corner and into a situation like that can easily increase your stress level and cause you to make decisions with very little time to think.

With that being said, try to remember not to tackle a situation like that by yourself if at all possible. Of course, there may be times when help is out of earshot and you will be the only adult present. In a situation like that, I would recommend that you run to the nearest classroom and let the teacher know what is happening, all the while screaming at the top of your lungs for those involved in the fight to break it up. That other teacher could send a trustworthy student for additional aid, and then that teacher would be free to join you in trying to stop the altercation.

Remember, while Chris was holding one of his two combatants up against a wall, he was completely vulnerable to attack himself. In fact, the other boy involved took advantage of that and continued to punch the boy Chris was holding! Chris could have very easily been injured himself. Remember, there's safety in numbers, so make as much noise as you can and look for help wherever possible.

Case Two

What Amy alludes to in her first example is one of the biggest problems facing an educator, and that is bullying. The fact that the young woman who was victimized lived in a foster home really had nothing to do with the fact that she was being targeted. The problem lies with those doing the bullying. Oftentimes their emotional needs are overlooked in the aftermath of such an event in favor of the victim's. After an appropriate disciplinary action has been handed out, all those involved should receive thorough attention from guidance counselors, school psychologists, or whatever form of student support is available. By addressing the root causes of the students' hostility, you stand a much better chance of preventing future events.

Amy's student teaching incident was a disaster waiting to happen. Never, ever should a student teacher be left alone, especially on her second day. Student teachers may come from the greatest school in the area and carry themselves like seasoned professionals, but the fact of the matter is they are not seasoned professionals. Their lack of experience alone should make this fact an obvious one, not even considering the possible legal ramifications involved. Amy's cooperating teacher left her in a dangerous situation. No student teacher should remain silent and allow their cooperating teacher to leave them alone. If this should ever happen, the student teacher should immediately let the cooperating teacher know it is not appropriate, and if necessary notify the school principal or college professor as well.

FINAL TIPS ON VIOLENCE

Speak up. The administration does not have the same access to student rumors and conversations as you do. While you may feel *positive* that a rumor is nothing, make a quick phone call to the principal's secretary and inform him or her of a possible problem, keeping the conversation free of speculation or your expert crime analysis, and hope that nothing comes of it.

The job doesn't end with the bell. While we are not suggesting that you don a cape and cowl and go looking for it, you may notice signs of trouble after your contractual day is done. Even though you are off the clock, you have a moral responsibility to call the school or local police if you notice something that stirs your sixth sense. Remember, it is always better to err on the side of caution.

Just as in our everyday lives, there is no surefire way to prevent every incident of violence that is going to occur in front of your eyes. However, if you know what to look for, you have a far greater chance of either preventing or minimizing those events. If you should be unfortunate enough to walk into the midst of an altercation, just remember to remain cool and understand that it is your job to do whatever is reasonably possible to bring the situation to a close. Of course, you are not bulletproof, so there are limits to what you will be able to accomplish, but bear in mind that the kids aren't bulletproof either, and you may be the closest thing to a hero around.

Luckily for Mrs. Opper, the day the school caught on fire was also the day she was teaching her home economics class how to make s'mores.

8

DON'T BRING
ME DOWN

As Dr. Watson so eloquently put it at Reichenbach Falls, it is with a heavy heart that this section is written. For you see, it was there that his friend and colleague Sherlock Holmes apparently plunged to his death, locked in a fatal embrace with that most evil of men, the Napoleon of Crime, Professor Moriarty. How fitting that the bane of Holmes's existence, that most insuperable of opponents, should be an educator. How bitterly tragic that the only way Holmes could defeat him was at the cost of his own life as well. And what is the point of this obscure reference from the public domain, you say?

Well, put simply, Holmes was remarkably educated, profoundly insightful, and dedicated to championing those in need. The only problem was that he was human (as human as a fictional character can be, of course). As brilliant as he was, there was still one opponent that he could not defeat and walk away from unscathed. This is how it will be for many of you, particularly those looking for their first jobs.

Where do most first-time educators end up that don't have an aunt that works in the local district office? It's a pretty safe bet to say that they will end up in the school systems of larger urban areas.

Please do not take this the wrong way, as teachers in city schools are some of the finest, most dedicated educators it will be your good fortune to ever work with. The problem with these systems is the seemingly endless lack of resources, a fact that has unfortunate consequences for the dedicated educator trying to do the best job humanly possible against such incredible odds. This lack of funding creates very serious by-products that can make your job much less about teaching and much more about surviving, sometimes quite literally, as you will read about later in this chapter.

Factors like insufficient numbers of staff, improper supervision of buildings, and oversized classes filled with kids to whom school is either the highlight of their day or a nightmare come to life will impact you in ways you never dreamed possible. In fact, the thought of returning to that place on a daily basis may be enough to make you cry. Things might be so bad that even the administration will give up. What's worse, your friends, relatives, fiancé, and anyone else remotely associated with you will probably give up on listening to your constant complaining about how bad that now mythical place is. If this section sounds a little frightening, there's a reason: It's supposed to.

Clearly, not all teaching situations are going to be as bad as the one previously mentioned, but what you do find is that most school systems seem to have some of these elements. What do you think happens to the so-called bad kids in an affluent suburb? Well, they have to go somewhere. It might even be the basement of the school they were supposedly kicked out of. That's just the way it is.

If you end up in one of these situations, you will undoubtedly wind up asking yourself why you continue to return to work at all. Sure, you could quit, and in many instances you probably should, but quitting isn't always as easy as it sounds, particularly when you consider the fact that you will no longer be receiving a paycheck, something that comes in pretty handy these days. And certain school systems frown on their teachers throwing up their hands in disgust and walking away from their kids, so if that system is the only game in town, be prepared to learn a whole new set of rules in another town. For many, quitting is just not an option.

So how does one survive such a dreary existence, when the very thought of the place creates a very uncomfortable feeling in your stomach and can keep sleep at bay for hours on end? Well, believe it or not, there are ways. You don't necessarily need to go over the falls, as Holmes did, as you try to fight through the deplorable conditions around you to reach the children waiting for you to guide them. It can be done, and it can be done without losing yourself along the way. Therefore, it is fitting that one final mention about the tragedy of Sherlock Holmes should be made, a fact that may give you a little hope in an otherwise hopeless situation. Yes, Holmes did confront Moriarty that day and yes, they both went over the falls. However, there is one important bit of information that I neglected to give you at the start of this section: *Holmes survived.* And so can you.

KNOW YOUR ENEMY

So how do you know if you're in a "bad" school? Trust us, you'll know. And for those who have not yet had the pleasure of strolling through one firsthand, it's probably best to understand why such places exist. We've all heard about them. The schools you should stay away from as if your life depended on it. Sadly, that simile is more like a fact in the present day. But the threat of violence is not the only factor that can define a school as "bad." We define a "bad" school as one where any of the following is taking place:

- The building and surrounding area are not safe.
- Little or no teaching is going on.

- Student behavior is out of control, and little or nothing realistic is being done about it.

Notice, we said that *any* of the above criteria help to define a "bad" school. And how are they measured? Well, let's take the first one. Violent acts that are reported to the proper authorities are recorded and have a nasty habit of being publicized at inopportune times and can give a school system and its administration a bad name. Some of us who have been at this for a while have often reported altercations we have witnessed to our immediate supervisors only to find out later that they were handled "in house" and not put "on the record." Now you know why.

What principal wants his or her school being called unsafe in the newspaper? Well, hopefully an honest one, but let's not forget that most principals were teachers themselves once so they have some idea of what life is like for the teachers they supervise. When managing a tough school with limited resources and staff, they often have to be creative in the methods they use to deal with problems, just as they were creative in the classroom in their younger days.

And let's face it, some schools are in pretty rough neighborhoods, where crime and violence is a common occurrence and parental influence is quite often nonexistent. So unless you plan to become a "Batman" like Joe Clark in *Lean on Me* and take the law into your own hands (which we do not recommend, by the way), accept the fact that bad things are going to happen in your school from time to time, or get another job.

A school where little or no teaching is going on? Those exist? Well, yes and no. Oftentimes, public perception plays a role in this one. For example, you could work in a nice, quiet, upper-class suburban area with a well-funded school system where everything seems to be going fine until the local newspaper publishes the standardized test scores for all the schools in the area, and

God help you if you are on the bottom of that list. Your area now becomes the "ghetto" of your county. Remember, as much as we may want to believe it, we can't all be winners, regardless of what the proponents of social promotion will tell you. Ultimately, someone has to make the bottom of that list. So does that make you a bad school? It depends on whom you ask.

The people at the top of the list would probably say yes; the kids in the real ghetto forty or fifty miles away would most likely say no and give up much of what they hold dear for the chance to learn in your "bad" school. Then again, there are schools where the instruction is quite poor, as your esteemed authors can attest to. Now, did those schools set out to hire the worst teachers possible to ensure that the student body received shoddy instruction? While some of us might want to answer yes to that question, it's a pretty safe bet that that is not the case. Instead, those schools are probably located in one of those challenging districts that have difficulty hiring the most qualified teachers available. Of course, that's not the only reason.

Let's face it. Students outnumber teachers by a ratio of what, twenty-five to one? Or thirty? Or thirty-five? If they really wanted to, they could turn the school upside-down. So why don't they? Well, many have tried, and with varying degrees of success. Ultimately, however, school buildings are still standing day after day and the waltz goes on. Unfortunately, your dance partner is not always into three-quarter time, and will let you know it. Clearly, they have not been practicing their steps at home. And while this may sound flippant, it's really not, for some of the most important steps in life are not being practiced at home.

Many new teachers take for granted the fact that parents are doing their part by teaching their kids the fundamentals, like respect for themselves and others, but sadly this is not always the case. And there are many reasons why, the most glaring of which is that there might not be anyone there to teach them anything beyond how to turn the television on and off while the parent is at work or the best way to get to school without getting jumped or worse.

Being polite to the teacher may not be high on many a child's list of priorities, and with little or no support from a parent to help back you up (and it's not just you; never forget that most of your colleagues are probably in the same boat), student comportment may be an issue. And the more time you spend trying to keep order, the more your instruction will suffer.

Are you thoroughly terrified? Are you ready to try law school again or take that job in your family's business? Well, if you plan to hang on, remember that this chapter deals with the most desperate of situations, and you know what they say about desperate times.

DESPERATE MEASURES THAT MAY HELP GET YOU THROUGH

Call 911. If something really bad is going down where people could get seriously hurt and you've reported it to your superiors and you still don't have faith in the school's ability to handle the situation, bust out that phone you've been paying way too much money for and call in the cavalry. That's what the police are there for. Just make sure you are willing to do your part and help the officers by naming names and giving specific details as to what occurred. While this may not endear you to a certain group of kids in your school (don't worry, it will with others), they may think twice before causing mayhem in your presence if they think it could get them arrested. And the embarrassment it causes the administration might encourage them to get off their duffs and spend a little more time in the halls to prevent this sort of thing from happening in the first place.

Document Everything. If a child says something totally outra-geous and inappropriate in class, write it down. Better yet, stop whatever it is you are doing and write it down in front of the whole class. When the student asks what you are doing, tell him. You will be reciting it word for word to his parent later that night on the phone. If Mom or Dad doesn't care, make sure it goes to an administrator. The same thing goes for physical confrontations you witness. A carefully documented play-by-play of everything that went down will be a great deal of help to the administration and, if need be, the police.

Become a Member of the Family. Do whatever you can to get par-ents involved. Call constantly. Send letters home. Wrangle a cell phone number or, better yet, a work number for them out of their child. If that doesn't work, find out who the child's emergency contact person is and harass them. A child throwing his or her chance at an education out the window counts as an emergency in our book. If you become enough of a burr under the saddle of the parents that are avoiding you, they might finally take action with their kid just to get rid of you.

Get to Know Your Kids. As scary as some of them may seem, they're still just kids. Talk to them about their lives. Find a way to relate to them. Try to mold your lessons around things that are important to them. In fact, learn about the things they care about and validate them. Showing a genuine interest in what they feel strongly about will gain you more points with those kids than any-thing else in the world. Let them know you care about them and you may be surprised at the response you get.

Never Take It Personally. You may feel like some of what is hap-pening is your fault and that you could be doing a better job. A kid may start screaming how much they hate you when you try to im-prove that kid's life by disciplining him or her. Frustrated parents or administrators may try to turn the tables on you with the old "Well, what are *you* doing to help the child stop this behavior?"

Don't buy into it. The fact that you work in this profession speaks volumes about you.

Blow Off Steam. Remember that sense of humor we told you to work on? It will come even more in handy the more absurd your situation seems to be. You may find yourself dealing with a lot of heavy-duty stuff on a daily basis, stuff you may not want to think about when you get home. Whatever you do, don't bottle it up. Don't try to suppress what you went through at work just because you survived another week and made it to the local bar. Remember, if you are under a great deal of stress and don't deal with it, it *will* come back to haunt you.

Know When to Fold 'Em. When complaining to a friend about the horrible work experience he was having, one of your illustrious authors was told something by that friend that really sums up this next point: "Nobody should have to take pills to go to work." This is a fact that one of us, unfortunately, had to deal with. No job is worth risks to your health. Again, this may seem obvious to some, but not to those who rely on the paycheck. Even if you do rely on the paycheck, bear in mind that there are other ways to make money in this world that a person with a teaching background can do without taking years off his or her life.

CASE STUDY

Chris Gets into Trouble at School and His Dad Has to Pick Him Up

We all have to start somewhere. After being teased with a four-month leave replacement in a school in Flushing, Queens, a school I was not asked back to, I soon found myself at Board of Education headquarters in Brooklyn, New York, on the second day of the new school year desperate for whatever opening I could find. I was quickly offered a job in the scenic Bronx not very far from my home in Queens. Okay, so I had to pay the toll on the Whitestone Bridge every day. It was worth it for a short commute. I accepted and soon found myself getting off the Bruckner Expressway for my first day at my new job. Of course, if I knew then what I know now, I probably would have just kept driving until my car hit the East River. But, not having the ability to see into the future, I put on my game face and leapt into it with two feet.

To be fair, the first month of the school year went pretty well. I was teaching seventh-grade Language Arts, and I was doing well. I mean, I had grammar lessons complete with overheads, good classroom control, and meetings with the parents of disruptive kids. I was on course for teacher of the year. Even the janitor, in his broken English, stopped during his duties one day to compliment me: "Hey, my friend."

"Yes?"

"You doing very good job."

"Thank you very much. I've been working very hard."

He continued as if he hadn't heard me: "Everything much better than last year."

The Vulcan in me should have raised an eyebrow at that one, but instead I wallowed in his compliments. After all, I was "superteacher": "Well, let's just hope it stays that way, huh?" He sort of half-smiled at that. Perhaps I knew more about the future than I thought.

Around the first week of October, things started to feel different. There was more noise in the hall than usual. The supportive parent of one of my more troublesome students stopped returning my calls. And worse, the principal, who had already been by for a patented New York City surprise observation, wasn't around as much as he used to be. He was being called down to his office more and more frequently over the school public address system. And more of my own students were starting to act out. It didn't make sense. Why were things changing?

This particular tale of mine could easily fill a book of its own, so I will spare you most of the gory details and get right to the point: The junior high school I had been sentenced to was being run by not only a first-year principal but a first-year assistant principal as well. And while they seemed to say and do all of the right things for the first few weeks, they soon became overwhelmed by the constant flow of behavior problems, mostly from the eighth and ninth grades, and it never seemed to let up.

Then word got out that the principal was, for want of a better word, a wimp. Stories of kids literally pushing him around in his own office spread like wildfire, and it wasn't long before legions of other kids started testing the boundaries of acceptability as well. With little or no support from the main office, the place quickly descended into chaos. As the old saying goes, cut off the head and the body dies. The rest of the faculty quickly started making their arrangements.

As the months went by, the behaviors I witnessed became harder and harder to comprehend. Bulletin boards were lit on fire. Florescent light fixtures were smashed on a daily basis. And toward the end of the year, when there was so little left to destroy, roving packs of children would team up (ordinarily a good thing) and, together, would rip the water fountains right out of the walls. I remember walking down on the first floor when my attention was seized by the soothing sound of trickling water. I looked up and found myself in an Esther Williams movie, watching the cool, clear water cascade down the steps in true MGM fashion. Were all of these things really happening? Frighteningly enough, yes. But they were nothing compared to the threats of physical violence.

Okay, I'm going to have to pull a dirty trick here and make you wait a bit before I continue with my previous point. I'm sure many readers are shaking their heads in disbelief and saying, "Why didn't this guy just quit?" Well, I almost did, many times, but ultimately did not, a choice I was glad I made, believe it or not. Here are the reasons why.

First and foremost, I had recently gotten engaged and now had a reception hall, a honeymoon, and most of the engagement ring to pay for. Even with those bills hanging over my head, however, I contemplated other avenues of employment. It was a chance encounter with one of my younger sister's high school teachers that convinced me otherwise.

I had substituted at my sister's high school a few times after graduating from college and became friendly with some of the staff there. It was about a year and a half later, while I was working in the Bronx, that I went to see my sister in her school play. I ran into one of her teachers, who remembered me, and we spoke briefly about how our respective jobs were going: "So, I hear you're up in the Bronx now. How's it working out?"

While you have been reading this book, you may have noticed that I try to inject some humor into the text whenever I can. That is also generally true of me in conversation, but it was not on that night. No, all talk about my work at that point had become devoid of humor. It was a topic I dreaded discussing, and I tried to simply put it out of my mind when I wasn't there. My once-sympathetic fiancée, the shoulder I literally cried on, let it slip that she was sick and tired of hearing about the Bronx. She quickly apologized, but I knew I was no longer my jovial self. I was a tired, bitter schoolteacher, and I was only in my first full year. So I responded to my sister's teacher as I responded to anyone that asked me about work at that point—bitterly: "It's absolutely terrible, man. The kids are out of control, the principal's useless, and I'm having trouble falling asleep at night. I'm thinking about quitting and trying to find a job in another school."

He looked at me and shook his head. I didn't realize it at the time, but his comments probably saved my teaching career: "You probably shouldn't do that. The city doesn't like it when people up and quit from tenure-track positions. It might keep you from getting another job in the system."

CHAPTER 8

In three seconds, my fantasies of having an escape route were smashed. I had been holding on to the fact that I could pull the old "take this job and shove it" line and walk out of that hellhole with some shred of dignity still in place. Now I discovered that I was in fact not in control of my destiny. That mysterious disembodied organism known as the Board of Education was. Granted, I could have looked for a job in a private school or outside of the city, but I had precious little experience and still held on to dreams of escaping to a high school, the place I really wanted to work. And not only that, what about having already survived all the pointless hoops the Board of Ed had made me jump through on my pathway to becoming licensed?

My favorite was driving to Brooklyn in a blizzard for the dreaded oral exam, in which I sat in an empty classroom with an intimidating proctor with a tape recorder and was asked how I would react to a number of stupid teaching scenarios. The whole situation had a ridiculous "secret society" air about it; the only thing missing was the blindfold and someone shooting beer cans off my head. Was I going to give up after going through all that? I made my choice. It now appeared that I was trapped in junior high, at least until June, and then I would make my move.

The months droned on and the stress level increased. I found myself spending my free periods covering for absent teachers because we couldn't get any substitutes to work there, particularly after that last guy got hit in the head with a battery. My lunch periods were spent locked in my classroom, where I would read old *Junior Scholastic* magazines that I found in a closet. I no longer brought in anything of great length to read, as I did not dare let my mind drift too far from where I really was. I learned my lesson the day I was lost in a Sherlock Holmes adventure. I didn't hear the jingling of keys outside the door and was ever the more shocked when an unfamiliar boy burst into what he thought was an empty room holding a ring full of school keys. He looked at me, smiled, and left. My stomach hurt.

Believe it or not, the end of this torment had begun to pull into view. It was now late May, and something glorious had happened in my life. Out of the blue, I received a letter from the Board of Ed that said they were anticipating a great deal of vacancies at the high school level the following year and would I mind coming to a hiring hall in Queens the day after school ended in June. Would I mind? Were they kidding? Then another thought came to mind: I started looking around my house for the hidden camera while wondering if Allen Funt was still alive. And the scary part was that I was serious. Anyway, I had my ticket out. I just had to make it to June. If only this pain in my stomach would go away.

As previously stated in this chapter, bottling up your emotions is not a good thing. Eventually, they find a way out, as I discovered in humiliating fashion. It was now mid-June and the end was in sight. Just two more weeks to go and I was a free man. Of course, there was no reason in the world why those final weeks should be anything but horrific, just like most of the others had been.

It was a relatively normal day. I got to my room in time to let my kids in before homeroom, as usual, and as I did, I noticed a boy in the hallway who wasn't supposed to be there. You see, the previous day, I had gotten this boy suspended. I haven't the foggiest idea what offense he was guilty of after all these years, but if it was good enough to get him thrown out of that place for five days, it must have been a doozy.

Anyway, there was this boy, who should not have been in school, leaning up against the wall of the hallway just outside my room and staring at me. He didn't say a word. He didn't have to. I'm sure he saw the fear in my face. I was caught completely off guard. Somehow, I was able to contact the dean of discipline (another lost memory) and the boy was escorted upstairs to his office.

About an hour later, I was asked to come to the dean's office, where the young man apologized to me. I mumbled something like "Okay" and went back downstairs. Around lunchtime, a few of my colleagues said they were going across the Bruckner to get some pizza and would I like to go. I said yes, looking forward to the relative fresh air outside of the building. I ate a slice while trying to look interested in the funny story my colleague was telling. As we left to go back to work, I felt the pain in the pit of my stomach again. Someone said, "Are you all right?" and I waved her off. I made it back to class, sat down, and waited for the bell to ring. Nanoseconds later it did, and then the trouble really began.

In their defense, the group of kids who came to class that period were a pretty nice bunch. I also had them as my homeroom class so I got to know them a little better than my other classes. The fact that they were nice kids wasn't the problem: The problem was that they were *kids*. As I sat behind my desk, one hand held over the pit of my stomach where the pain was coming from, I was deluged with requests to go to the bathroom, to put the work on the board, and a million other things I can't remember. What I do remember was the difficulty I was having drawing breath, the sudden feeling of claustrophobia that was setting in, and the desire to hurl myself out the nearest window. Instead of answering their questions, I asked them for help.

A few moments later, one of my kids had returned with a recently hired assistant principal, a well-meaning woman sent to help clean up this school beyond help. She took over my class and suggested I have a seat in the teachers' lounge. I accepted her offer. As I sat there, the other teachers in the room could tell that something was seriously wrong with me, particularly when I tried to speak and couldn't, hyperventilating instead. I soon found myself in the principal's office, where the well-meaning but completely out-of-place man tried to make me feel better. I was obviously done working for the day, and as I got up to walk out of the building, I suddenly got dizzy and had to sit down again. The secretaries suggested I call someone to pick me up and that I was in no condition to drive. I uncharacteristically agreed with them and called my daddy to pick me up from school.

Instead of going home we went straight to the doctor's office. Fortunately, my fiancée and future wife, Tara, worked there, so I didn't have to wait long. After an EKG was performed and several questions were answered, I was told that I was suffering from an anxiety disorder and had been initiated into the wonderful world of panic attacks. A few days and one endoscopy later, I discovered I had an ulcer. When I told the doctor how stressful my job was, he told me to quit. I did not. Thanks to some pharmaceutical help I got through the next few weeks and made it to the hiring hall in Queens. Finally, I had gotten what I wanted: I was appointed to a high school. I had to go through Hell to get there, but I did it. The question I still, to this day, have difficulty answering is whether or not it was worth it.

ADMINISTRATIVE ANALYSIS

Charles Dickens wrote in *David Copperfield*, "In a school carried on by sheer cruelty, whether it is presided over by a dunce or not, there is not likely to be much learnt." For some teachers, the opposite may hold true—when students display cruelty or misbehavior, nothing can be taught. In the media of the twentieth and twenty-first centuries, public schools have been portrayed as cruel and oppressive. In films from *The Blackboard Jungle* to *The Breakfast Club,* the teachers in public schools have been portrayed as ineffective or clueless as to the students' values and needs. As a matter of course, the new teacher in a public school is served up as a spineless idealist or sarcastic dictator. The students are portrayed as clichéd pieces of a misunderstood youth culture.

In reviewing Chris's experience, the perception becomes reality. The culture of an urban public school can be a mirror of both what we believe and what we experience in concert with the media's exploitation of public schools. Students are cruel, the administration is invisible, and teaching becomes nonexistent or an act of desperation. The mission is to escape or be oblivious. Neither really works if we are to be effective as teachers.

Effective, if not exemplary teaching, can take place in a setting where such a reality as Chris's exists. Case studies done in the late 1980s by the Council of the Great City Schools outline strategies that support teachers like Chris to continue as effective teachers despite the circumstances around them. In collaboration with those studies, the experiences of countless teachers in diverse settings allow us to draw some general conclusions about success in today's public schools.

First and foremost, every school is a community and every classroom a community within that larger setting. The first task of any new teacher is to establish an understanding of the community members. In Japanese culture, teachers before the start of the year visit the homes of their students, talking with both student and parent about the classroom experience. In village schools throughout Cambodia, teachers hold regular meetings with parents collectively before the students enter the classroom.

The reality in America is that we subscribe to a "drop in and abide by my rules syndrome." To be successful we must have a clear understanding of the environment these children will come from. Our job is not to mimic that environment or duplicate it, but to use that understanding to communicate and create a classroom environment that is safe and nurturing.

A call to parents, a meeting with students individually prior to the classroom experience, a walk through the neighborhood, will change the perception that this is just another classroom.

How we direct our perceptions, how we respond, and what we value are modeled every moment we are in a child's presence. The environment of the classroom and the hallway must reflect your understanding and values regarding community along with a respect for the autonomy of the world outside.

For example, gang activities in schools have been neutralized by reaching an understanding that the school represents neutral ground. The school represents a set of values understood to be different than that of the streets. In a classroom and a hallway, this means neither the teacher nor the student will adopt behavior that violates that premise. To curse is unacceptable for both student and teacher. If we have an understanding that the school is a separate community, where expectations are clearly drawn, then a safe environment can and will be created. As a teacher, that place of community can only be controlled within the classroom, even as the environment around may be in chaos.

Within a subject as complex as teaching within a diverse public setting, there are many processes by which community can be achieved. What students look for in developing a sense of purpose is modeled by the teacher. One may ask, just how committed are you? If you have one foot out the door, so do I. If you communicate to me in an inappropriate way because I have done so, then it is fair to assume that such communication is appropriate at any time. If you model sarcasm about the system, then the system does not deserve respect from me as a student. These are extraordinary messages. If we communicate more positive messages effectively, we are able to build a community of effective learners. If not, we teach to a cynical, disinterested community reflective of a distrusting media and exacerbate quick escapes from our idealism as teachers.

FINAL TIPS FOR GETTING THROUGH THE TOUGH SITUATIONS

If you find yourself in a difficult teaching situation, remember that you don't have to stay there for life. If it's just not happening in one school, leave it and find another. Find out if your school district has a system in place that allows teachers to transfer to other schools. If the problems you left behind appear in your new school, try again. And if you find that it's just too tough wherever you go, then perhaps you should consider earning that paycheck of yours some other way, at least for a little while. Taking a step back from the profession can allow you time to go back to school and work on things that you may have had trouble with. Remember, as long as people keep having babies, the profession will be waiting for you when you're ready to return.

CONCLUSION

When young children are asked what they want to be when they grow up, some of the more popular answers they give are a police officer, a firefighter, or a teacher. It's interesting to note that, right up there with the people that protect us from bad guys and fires, are the people that give us homework and make us spit out our gum.

Why would the teacher be included in that group? Teachers don't get to wear a uniform or carry handcuffs or wear a really cool hat. What's the allure to a child? Well, in the eyes of a child, teachers are there to help and protect them, just like police officers and firefighters. And teachers do wear a uniform. It may not be as impressive as those worn by first responders, but it exists. It may be the pocket protector one teacher in particular always has in his shirt or the holiday-themed sweaters always worn by another. And teachers are first responders too. It makes no difference if a student suffers a skinned knee or is suffering through his or her first day back in school after a family tragedy.

In addition to education, the teacher is there to provide the comfort and support children need. It doesn't matter if the student is in kindergarten or graduating high school. When something bad happens, whether it is a personal matter or something on a global scale, they will look to you to be their rock, to help them make sense of it, to let them know that there is someone there to look out for them. That is the part of the job you don't learn in an education course.

We all know the old saying that teenagers know everything. Well, that statement also applies to teachers, at least in the eyes of their students. Think about the shock you felt the first time you saw one of your childhood teachers misspell a word on the blackboard or forget the name of a character in a story. You were shocked by your teacher's fallibility because, believe it or not, students hold teachers in very high esteem. You will be somewhat larger-than-life in your students' eyes, and as a result you have a responsibility to maintain that image.

That doesn't mean you have to read every book ever written or solve complex mathematical equations in record time. What it means is you have to be more than someone who lectures and takes attendance. You have to understand that these kids are yours to nurture during the course of the school day even when you don't feel much like nurturing. You have to understand that you may have the greatest job in the world. Saying that you get to mold the minds of tomorrow's leaders may sound cliché but it's true. You have the chance to educate children in more ways than one. In fact, a great deal of a child's moral code may be shaped by the way his or her teachers present themselves in the classroom.

Of course, there will be tough times, but remember that life can be quite tough, regardless of where you work or how much money you make. And not everyone is going to love you. One of the most vicious and baseless slurs that has ever been crafted to injure an entire group of people is "Those who can't, teach." Unfortunately, there are many ignorant people in this world that see the teacher as nothing more than an overpaid baby-sitter with summers off, particularly when the time to negotiate a new contract comes around. Issues like this one may be a sad by-product of our profession, but we, as educators, cannot allow ourselves to have our spirits broken by those who know nothing about the difficult work we do. It's just one more obstacle for the teacher to overcome.

Throughout this book, we have tried to point out some of the challenges the new teacher will face, but never forget the fact that there will always be new challenges. Don't let that fact scare you; let it motivate you. The rewards far outweigh the difficulties. You may teach the same subject matter for thirty years and have a completely unique experience with it each year.

You will have the opportunity to laugh and cry and learn with hundreds, perhaps thousands, of some of the most interesting people you will ever meet. You will educate, you will inspire, and you will be loved for it. You may not see that love right away, but we guarantee you will while waiting on line in the supermarket or when you are getting your oil changed or wherever you happen to be when a former student recognizes you and thanks you for being such a great teacher. The way you will feel inside when that happens is almost too difficult to describe. It will be a combination of joy, pride, and accomplishment. How many other professions can offer the same?